The Blue Collar Manifesto

Freedom in the 21st Century requires an accurate view of reality

The Blue Collar Manifesto

Freedom in the 21st Century requires an accurate view of reality

by
Richard Talmadge Conken

First Edition: February 2014
Printed in the United States of America
ISBN:-13: 9781496169235

Contents

Preface

My original plan was to have the psycho-babble at the front of the book. This information explains, 'how we acquire our sense of reality', and like bird watching, can be fascinating, but for most people, is usually not. So, in the spirit of being honest, let's just admit that kind of subject matter can be a difficult read. That's why it is now at the end of the book.

However, as mind numbing as this kind of dry information can be, it does not reduce its critical importance to you. Everybody should know how they acquire their version of reality and how that view will affect their life. It is equally important to understand a person's reality can be manipulated for good or harm.

Feel free to jump ahead to the last chapter if you see a term you would like to better understand.

Chapter One

Recognizing Thinking Errors

If they can manipulate your opinion they can manipulate your reality

There exists within you a powerful species survival tool that will prompt you to dismiss everything I'm about to say. My counseling curriculum taught me about this survival tool and the same science taught the powerful people who are using it against you. I'm doing more here than to just give you a 'heads up'. I'm trying to help you escape.

If you hang with me and try to hear me accurately, without justifying yourself or your current views, in just three or four hours, I will change your world. I will put you on a path to recover a thing taken from you. Control of your life.

What you need to know, first and foremost, is simply human logic is not always as logical as we would like to believe. I'm going to save the psycho-babble for the last chapter. So for now, let's open this discussion with the common thinking errors we all can fall into. To help flesh this out I'm going to use information found in a book given to me years before I entered the counseling program. When I first read it nothing made much sense so I put it down.

A few days before graduation I went looking it. To my surprise, apparently not everything I read, was forgotten. With the background provided by the counseling curriculum everything now made sense. And more than that, much of the content seemed remedial.

When, "The Fifth Discipline, the art and practice of the learning organization", was published, Dr. Peter M. Senge was the Director of the Systems Thinking and Organizational Learning Program at MIT's Sloan School of Management. I'm going to borrow and adapt his descriptions of 'learning disabilities'. The therapist may use a different term, 'thinking errors'. Also, don't be insulted. We all have them. In this very complex world we live in, learning disabilities and other types of thinking errors, can be expected. It is helpful to know they exist. Understanding we have them will help explain some of the mess we've gotten ourselves into.

Learning Disabilities: Thinking perspectives we need to overcome.

1. "I am my position"

It is so easy to identify ourselves with the thing we do for a living. "I'm a IBEW wireman." "I B in Everybody's Way." "I've Been Every Where." "I'm Broke Every Wednesday." "I Block Every Walkway." "International Brotherhood of Electrical Workers."

Often, we give focus to our role at work at the expense of our role in greater society. Our work, this small part we occupy in the world is easier to manage mentally, than the social issues facing us all. To that end, we tend to identify with a social philosophy encased within a political party. "I am a Democrat." "I am a Republican."

Too often we just stop there. As it relates to learning and reality, we shortchange ourselves. It becomes enough for our side to be better than the other side. Because we trust our side we don't feel the need to challenge our team. This is a learning disability. We assume our team, not only is looking out for us, but it also has the wisdom to do it in such a way that it brings us no harm.

We need to move beyond that. We need to move beyond having a stakeholder mentality, that is to say, "I have a stake in the future you are creating". A stockholder mentality would do us much better. "I own stock in my country. This is my money. I'm watching how well you perform. If you don't do a good job I will fire you." We need to lift our collective noses off the grindstone long enough to see where we are heading and how well our political money managers are doing. We need to expand 'our position'.

2. "The enemy is out there"

Up at the top, my opening remark spoke to a phenomenon therapists understand as 'Proposition 16'. It translates as, "I know I'm right, and I'm not so sure about you right now, so back off!" This aspect of human nature creates a learning disability. If we know we are right, then it follows, somebody else is wrong. As it relates to the team sport we know as politics, the other guys are the enemy. This makes perfect sense to us.

Hence, the learning disability. We leave ourselves with absolutely no room to learn. We trust at the expense of learning. It gets worse; in actuality, because we trust, we also learn what our side would have us to learn. They can tell us, 'this is the way it is', and we will adopt their view, most of the time without question. This thinking error leaves us at a huge disadvantage. To trust the intentions of our side is one thing.

To trust the wisdom of our side to pull it off without doing us harm is another. Huge Huge Difference.

3. "The illusion of taking charge"

This speaks to the issue of being proactive. "Damn it, this is our time. Now is when we need to speak with one voice and make our voice heard." Every election cycle we hear the same cry for solidarity. The problem becomes a problem when we think we are being 'proactive', when closer inspection, would prove we were being 'reactive'. We vote a certain way as a reaction to our fears concerning what would happen if the other side was in power. Senge offered, "true proactiveness comes from seeing how we contribute to our own problems." "(Proactiveness) is a product of our way of thinking, not our emotional state".

Consider this example to be one way we contribute to our own problems. Our whole political process is rooted in this reality. We vote with our pocketbooks. We vote for pork. The seniority system in the Senate and Congress is such that the longer you are in, the more power you have, and the more pork you can send home. As a nation, we have yet to learn this is not a good way to run a country. All of our fiscal problems stem from this approach to self-governance. We have yet to connect the dots accurately. We have poisoned our own water. It is that serious.

4. "The fixation on events"

Our adult rational mind is designed to analyze the information in front of us. Its purpose is make decisions as to how we are to relate within the current environmental field. As such, it is not designed to take in the big picture. Rather, it will deal with immediate imagery and context provided. Thus, we 'leap before we look'. We deal with the snapshot and not the documentary. We fixate on events.

Back in the day, when Saber Tooth Tigers viewed us a food source, this design feature came in very handy. We saw, we reacted, and if quick enough, we survived. Senge, speaks of the irony of this feature. "Today, the primary threats to our survival, both of our organizations, and societies, come not from sudden events but from slow, gradual processes."

To understand your reality accurately, you need to make allowances for this design feature. Certainly, the reality manipulators who seek your vote, will do everything in their power to cause you to fixate on events, rather than help you understand the slow gradual process as to how the event occurred in the first place. And, sometimes they will cause you to fixate on one event just to keep your eye off another, more important, event quietly brewing. This is political gamesmanship 101.

5. "The boiled frog"

This issue speaks to the slow, gradual processes of change, which eventually create circumstances in our society, that demand our immediate attention. We see them as a crisis when they first appear on our radar. Senge provides the image of a frog swimming in a pot of water on the stove. Heat the water up slowly and the frog will adapt all the way up to the time it boils to death. To perceive your reality clearly you need to understand what it is you are adapting too. The slow process of adapting creates the learning disability. We never wonder if there is a downside to 'adapting'. We never go there. We should. We just don't.

One of many things the American people have adapted to are our elected leaders and privileged press lying to us. No one seems to question whether or not politicians or their friends in

11

the press willfully misrepresent the truth. We should and the greater question which begs to be asked is, "how close to the boiling point are we?" "How much room for adapting is left?" We have even adapted to allow the leaders of our side to lie but draw the line when the other side does it. We won't allow our husband or wife to lie to us. We won't allow our Business Agent to lie to us. Why should we allow our elected officials?

6. The delusion of learning from experience

The issue at hand is not that we don't learn from experience. We certainly do. The 'delusion' aspect comes from two crucial areas. First, as this relates to 'thinking errors', some things we have learned are just not accurate. Examples are seen in every aspect of life. We can learn good things and we can 'learn lies'. And, we can 'learn' to trust manipulative people. This kind of learning works as a delusion. As a result we will never experience the promised outcome. Nor, will we connect the dots to understand why.

Another form of delusion is revealed in the consequence of applying the things we have learned from experience. This has nothing to do with accuracy or honesty. This has to do with time. When we make decisions based only on our experience, oftentimes we will not recognize or even be around when the final consequences play out. We make decisions anticipating intended consequences. Unintended consequences are far more difficult to predict. The delusion arises in believing we solved the problem when, in actuality, we created a much bigger one. Sometimes, we never connect the dots. Time passes, the problem appears, and we cannot recognize our fingerprints all over it.

I'm a blue collar working class guy who has been taught to assess reality accurately. I've been trained to be a reality engineer. As such I see reality manipulation where other

12

people are blind to it. How could they? To my blue collar working class brothers and sisters, this thing I'm doing, is my way of saying, "I've got your back".

This is also my way of saying, "I'm angry" and I want you to feel the same way. The way I see it, it is our friends, the people we blindly trust, who have done us the most harm. And, it is ugly. We can and must make them stop. We need to accurately see what it is they have done and what it is they are doing. This is not about intentions. This is not about the other guys messing things up. You will see it is about our side and their policies and the bad consequences they've brought into our home.

It is my intention to spank the Progressive Democrats. The Republicans we know about. The Progressive Democrats, our friends, these folks are the ones we need to take to the woodshed. We hired them to be our advocate, to look out for us while we stayed on the job to earn a living. We hired them based on a 'perceived alliance'. We hired them on promised intentions, when we should have looked more closely at the wisdom and the predictable consequences to their policies. And, this lesson we should learn, we would do well to distinguish between a perceived alliance and an actual one.

The work of the politician is similar to what we see in construction. We build things. So, do they. As a teenager I was given this admonition by my great-grandfather. He told me to ALWAYS do 'pretty work'. He equated the quality of the work with the character of the man. He told me that I would never be able to hide my work. Even if it was covered, within the walls, it would eventually be seen by someone. This is true for politicians as well.

When you learn how to see reality clearly. You will be able to see some really shoddy work done by our politicians. Both

13

political parties. You will be able to see the excessive amount of energy they use to keep the consequences of their work hidden and invisible to us. You and I know the best time to fix a mistake is the moment we first recognize it. Stop everything, take it off the wall, do it over. That kind of thinking is beyond them.

No doubt you've worked with guys who didn't get it. Their work would come loose on the wall or fall off the ceiling. And, to make matters worse, they would lie like it wasn't their work at all. If you've been there then you know what would happen next. They would be run off and we'd have to fix it. This is our situation today. Our politicians have done crappy work that created crappy consequences and they are doing everything in their power to keep it hidden. We need to run them off. And, we need to step up and fix it.

And another thing. Blue collar workers, not all, but way too many of us suck at doing relationships. This thing is nearing epidemic proportions. The tools I provide in the last section will help you interpret both realities. The real time social/political issues as well as the real time relationship ones. As it is true in the social/political realm, it is also true for relationships, it is crucial for you to recognize what it is you are doing that contributes to your own problems.

It has been observed the reason America has such a high divorce rate is because the skill set necessary to enjoy a successful, committed, long term relationship is being erased from public memory. This is the boiled frog thing again. We can adapt to social change regardless if it is healthy for the individual or the species. Right now one thing we know is broken relationships are not healthy for the individuals or the family's involved. There may come a time when the species informs us it cannot survive continual broken relationships. This could happen and we may be seeing the effects within

14

our society today.

I'm going to do by best to teach you how to question your version of 'normal'. I really hope I'm successful. Everything I'm trying to accomplish hinges of that.

All of our reality takes place within a small section of our brain. I want to show you it can be tweaked for the better or the worse. And, I want to show you that it has already been tweaked; without your permission and to your detriment. I could say you are a victim of psychological warfare. It is that serious. So, when you hear me talk about helping you escape, understand this is where you are being held captive.

Come along with me and learn a more accurate way to perceive reality or go to your grave captive and uninformed. No arm twisting. Choose door number one or door number two.

Chapter Two

A More Accurate View of Reality

just because this is the way things are doesn't mean it has to be
just because this is the way things are doesn't mean it really is this way

I would trust 550 working class grandmothers to lead this nation over the group we have in Washington right now. I think I could believe in their collective wisdom. I think I could trust their values. Would you agree we've come to the place where what we have is not working anymore? This section will help you understand why it is this way and how it became this way.

I remember the time I stood three feet away from a healthy, young adult Golden Eagle. Majestic. Proud. Regal. Beautiful. A perfectly designed hunting machine in the prime of his life. Yet, there was a chain attached to his leg.

It is believed he was taken out of his nest and raised in a cage. When he grew too large for the cage he was then taken to the local woods and released. On the day of his capture, he was in a small Colorado mountain town doing things Golden Eagles are not supposed to do. He walked up to humans and begged for food.

When he was removed from the nest, he was cheated out of knowing the full essence of what it means to be a Golden Eagle. The important 'how to survive in the wild like eagles do' information was not transmitted from his parents to him. He did not know how to fend for himself. His rules and tools were woefully lacking. He was taught to be dependent on man.

This state was his normal. He looked like an eagle. He could make little baby eagles. But, he did not possess the important 'eagle knowledge' to pass on to his children. So, was he an eagle as his species defines, "eagle"? I don't think so. He looked like an eagle, but he couldn't live like an eagle.

You may have already guessed where I'm heading. There exists a full essence of what it means to be human. And for most of us, because we were taught to focus on other things, we have been cheated out of experiencing just what that means.

The poor and the powerless have always had it rough. Life is hard now but it shouldn't be THIS hard. It may be worse for the poor and working class family today than at any other time in history. We live in a world where technology and ideology and power and arrogance and betrayal have merged and now exist as a unified force to do us, the working class folks, the most evil kind of harm. Chains are being attached to us and they feel like normal.

It is because I've earned the degree in Counseling, received the training that makes me a reality engineer, completed the curriculum that taught me to analyze personal and social reality, I can know we are in deep deep trouble.

And, it is because I'm blue collar through and through, lived a lifetime with less, struggled financially from day to day, month to month, year to year, and familiar with the situations that cause people from time to time to seek a soft place to land, I can say, I'm one of you. We will always have a bond even if we never meet.

And, I know this to be true. Without this information, you cannot know you are being systematically enslaved. You cannot know you are blind. You cannot know you are lost. You cannot know you are being harvested by the people and institutions you trust. There is no reason for you to know. Who would teach you? This information is too valuable. The information you need to protect yourself has been purposely withheld. "Knowledge is power" remember?

Understanding The Problem

Without technology Hitler could not have changed the way the German people of Aryan descent felt about the Jewish citizens as quickly as they did. Radio and print media of the day bombarded the nation with a common and consistent message and effectively altered the way the regular citizens of Germany thought. If they didn't buy into it then they were intimidated enough to keep quiet. A win for Hitler.

Today, science can explain how it worked and this you will come to understand. For now, just realize the communicative powers available to affect how you feel about anything are 100 times more effective than the tools Hitler used.

Hitler's ideological message was simple. The Aryan race is superior and Germany must remove any impurities as to keep the race pure. The philosophy from which to publish his ideology is more basic. "I have the means to change the way our citizens think and I should use it". Hitler's success has not escaped the attention of the leaders of the "progressive" movement. They have the power now and are in the 'change the way you think business'. When Obama spoke and promised a "change you can believe in" his actions prove he had every intention to use the Hitler model. Our First Lady was downright giddy when she spoke about a visible' cultural shift' working it's way through America. She was claiming victory.

Power. Nothing gets done without power. Progressive and liberal democrats have long held the positions of power in Politics, Journalism and Education. They have functionally controlled the 'message' Americans received for my entire lifetime, and most certainly yours. The reason they have not been more influential was simply their views were too extreme. There were too many Americans who disagreed with them. The common everyday folks held the ballot box power. The progressive message could be contained. A thing to disagree with.

Now, this group of Americans are dying out. Only a remnant remains. They have a common memory of a different America and we know them collectively as the Tea Party. Progressive educators, journalist, and media personalities have attacked, in the rudest fashion, them and their views. The Hitler message that attacked the Jews is very similar to those used to attack our oldest living citizens. "They are the reason for all our problems and we don't want them among us". What worked for Hitler will work for the progressives if they remain in power. We can strongly disagree with everything the tea partiers stand for. We should not stand quietly by and allow our oldest living citizens to be insulted this way.

Arrogance. One meaning for this term is to trust your conclusions without allowing challenge for accuracy. Progressives want to create social change without regards to the negative consequence. They actually believe they are smart enough to 'create a better world'. Unfortunately for the majority of Americans, the progressives have at their disposal the means for changing the culture in our country. To be fair, not everything they do or did is bad.

Their shining moment came exposing racial prejudice, bigotry, and its associated injustice. Their victory was just partial though. The consequence that followed may have been intended or unintended. Here's what happened. Through the constant barrage of the ugly, racist, white person bigot imagery, intended to stop that wrongful behavior, a new shift in bigotry emerged. Now, the only true racism in America is black on white bigotry. Or, perhaps we can add the new development, Hispanic on white bigotry. Of course we have to pretend there is no Black on Hispanic bigotry or vice versa.

We've reached the place where the progressive intention is visible. It has become clear they are encouraging animosity between the ethic groups within our country. The progressives used their tools to win the war against racism in America and then brought it back. For a while we had a chance. Now, we are being ripped apart as a nation and re-segregated socially. An 'us against them', you need me, motif is provided as the only way to survive. "Vote for the democrats and they will save you".

The progressive democrats are arrogant. "Progressive" translates as "society creator" and they refuse to acknowledge any misstep or negative consequence associated with any of their grand 'I am smarter than you' social engineering schemes. How could we ever know. The progressives control the media and have convinced a majority of Americans any alternative message source, like talk radio or Fox News, are racist, bigoted, anti-working family, outside the mainstream, not good for America, homophobe's. Progressives will never admit to any wrongdoing or negative consequence to their social engineering. They always deflect blame and responsibility and they destroy people who oppose them.

Betrayal. Our government was established from one guiding intention: to protect the people of the United States from tyrants both foreign and domestic. Special privilege was conferred onto the press. The implied understanding suggests they would be the outside observer to expose any and all wrongdoing by our elected officials. The American people have been betrayed by every wing, by every faction, of the Press.

Fox news could have helped. But, they appear satisfied just having a large audience, the 'Republican' viewer. Broadcasting is just business to them. They don't want to educate. They half-step. They just want to pat us on our heads and say... nothing to change the status quo. Nobody at Fox is looking out for you. If anyone at Fox thinks they are looking out for us, then, perhaps they should review, their definition for what that means.

When an American President looks the people in the eye and lies to them and he does it often, as Obama does, and knows he will get a pass, and will never be held accountable, then we are doubly betrayed. I should point out if you feel comfortable with the President lying then your 'normal' is to be dishonest or your reality has been morphed to accept the notion President's are allowed to lie. We never should have a leader lie to us and we never should have a press that is willfully working with him to mislead us. Period!

Consider the following and compare it to what you've been told to believe:

Big oil is responsible for the high price of gasoline.

Not true. The Press, the Democrats, AND the Republicans

have betrayed us. The reason gas is so high is directly related to the number of refineries processing the oil. The main issue was never about drilling for oil. That, very visible, in the public 'debate', is just smoke and mirrors. A distraction. The high price of gasoline has always been about refining capacity.

For decades our refineries have been operating up to 95% capacity or greater. Any kind of gulf storm will affect the process, diminish the supply, and the price at the pump will spike. It has been observed we should be operating at a maximum of 60 to 65% capacity. If that were the case, the price at the pump could get down to around $2.00 a gallon. Now you can make excuses or ask the obvious questions.

Why is this situation allowed to continue? And, where is the extra money going? I can only suspect money is the reason and the bulk of the profit is going to the stockholder politicians and media moguls that are encouraging this to occur. When you hear me say we as a people are being harvested this is just one example. Think about how much extra you alone are spending on gas. Multiply it by 200 million. That is a lot of money.

Predatory lenders caused the mortgage crisis.

This is the story repeated over and over by the main stream media. Not true and this is what happened. The Progressives wanted to level the playing field for poor Americans and help them buy a home in their pursuit of the American dream. A good thing with horrible consequences. They put a law through Congress. It essentially said the American tax payer will co-sign any and every mortgage that met a qualifying standard so low the banking industry professionals labeled as a train wreck doomed to happen. And it did happen.

With the media's help a story was developed and passed off as true which placed all the blame on predatory lenders. Of course, these lenders were put in business by Congress. They followed the rules written by Congress. Oversight was the responsibility of Congress. Billions of dollars were lost and the arrogance of the Progressive Democrat is by and far the supreme reason our country went into this awful recession. The writing was on the wall years before the bottom fell out.

Obama had no choice.

He had to borrow massive amounts of money in an attempt to spend our way out of the recession. NOT! Today hundreds of millions of dollars cannot be accounted for. The truth is, Obama did have a choice. He could have put America back to work. If we had a Press who cared for America and her people you would have heard about it. The need for refineries is not my secret. Most reasonable people believe we ought to be energy independent. We certainly would have more money to spread throughout the economy if the price of gasoline dropped $1.50 a gallon. This aspiration alone would have united the country.

It is obvious the Democrats really do not care about the working class, union or otherwise. Obama could have followed the model of another progressive, FDR. President Roosevelt put the nation to work through the building of roads, bridges, parks, and dams. Obama as President choose to print obscene amounts of money and create a giveaway program we know as the Federal Unemployment Extension. Brilliant! With the same money he could have began the process toward energy independence.

Instead of a handout, working men and women could have build enough refineries, oil pipelines, nukes, conventional powerhouses, and all the associated manufacturing to supply this endeavor, and make energy independence a reality. He could have put organized labor to work. That action alone would have brought the rest of the nation up and running in less than a year. Think about it. During this time, organized labor limped along with over 25% of their members out of work. I knew apprentices, who at the end of their first year, had zero work hours in the craft. It did not have to be that way. I had an apprentice in his third year of school that did not have enough hours to get out of his first year.

What? Union brothers are OK with that? Is that what we do? Eat our dead and sacrifice our young just to keep progressive democrats in office? Quit thinking like it is 1965. They blew their chance and should not be rewarded for it. I'm not saying the other side is better. I'm saying we should recognize our power within our two party system and use it to tell both of them how we want our world to look. If the Republicans hear us first, then maybe we should give them a chance. We have the power and we should not continue to waste it. We are working men. There is work that needs to be done. We don't ask for much. Just point us in the direction of the work and turn us loose.

America needs to understand, organized labor excels at building the Big and the Massive: refineries, pipelines, nukes, and powerhouses. Multi-year projects. This is what we do. We don't build stick houses. We build powerhouses. Labor and America were thrown under the bus by this arrogant progressive. Somewhere in all this 'Obama Wisdom' is the true reason he was nominated for the Nobel peace prize after just eleven days in office. He has an agenda and it does not appear to be in the best interest of the America you and I live in. Hardly a peep out of the press.

Obama uses his power to help black people.

NOT! The ugliest thing Obama did was to turn his back on

24

African-Americans and the American Black Family. There is a huge difference between what he says and that which he does. What happened makes the Tuskegee syphilis experiments, as horrendous as they were, compare as almost governmental playfulness.

The American government willfully experimented on the American Black Family on a National scale.

Understand in 1965 Congress was actually trying to do a good thing. The crime was not in their attempt to fix a god awful problem. The crime lies in their arrogance and refusal to dismantle, pull out by the roots, undo, just make go away this calamity that continues to this day.

Therapists and the progressive social architects agree, in the course of human existence, everything we do can be viewed as an experiment. With every action we set in motion a consequence that invariably must follow. This is straight systems thinking. Maybe you will remember a thing I learned in school. When formed, our government was known throughout the western world as the "Great Experiment".

Certainly this concept is common knowledge at the congressional level, wouldn't you think? So, every politician should know when they create a new social structure, a new law, it is guaranteed to create a consequence. Typically, a law does not pass without writing it in such a way as to guarantee the intended consequence. Now, let's see what they did for Black Americans.

Congress wrote a law history shows was clearly directed toward the black community. Written by the best minds of the progressive movement this law effectively told young black women if they took the plunge, and had a baby without being married, the government would provide them with food, clothing, housing, utilities, and spending money... forever. It would only stop if and when they got married.

It doesn't matter so much about intentions or what the government actually said. What matters is, what the people actually heard and what actually happened. Systems theory tells us the intention of the law might well have been to destroy the American Black Family, or perhaps The American Family, because that is exactly what it is doing.

Two related events happened in my life I would like to share. In 1969, just four years after this law passed, I was in high school chatting with a group of fellow seniors. We were floating our plans for after graduation. Work for daddy. Join the service. Go to college. Get married. A voice from beside me said, "I'm going to have a baby". "The government will give you money and an apartment if you have a baby as long you don't get married." "I might have two because they give you more money".

Have my own apartment? An enticing thought for any teenager. Still, I could not fully process the notion a girl would deliberately set out to get pregnant. This was 1969. We did not think that way. Understand this. That kind of thinking, which was foreign in my world, had already established a foothold in hers. Was she a bad person? No! People can do just about anything if the apparent social approval deems the behavior to be normal and acceptable. Look at pre-WW2 Germany.

In 1985 I had the responsibility to invite guest speakers to our Saturday morning men's fellowship breakfast. I telephoned a black inner-city pastor and after awhile he agreed to my request. On the scheduled morning he arrived, and showed himself to be friendly, but somewhat distracted. He was burdened by the events of the previous night.

He proceeded to air out his thoughts and feelings. You may know it is common for sermons to begin with a rhetorical question. And this is how he started, even before we sat down, "Are your babies having babies?" "Are your young girls having babies without being married?" I think I knew right away he wasn't preaching. He was trying to make sense out of a new phenomenon erupting within his sense of normal. This man exhibited a true pastor's heart and it was obviously breaking.

He told us he had spent most of the previous evening with a family trying to come to grips with just how their little girl, would do a thing, her parents and her pastor thought to be, unthinkable. Had these folks possessed the skills of the reality engineer, they would have known. They would have had something or someone to blame. The eight or nine white men in the room couldn't offer any real help. We were all blue collar. How could we know?

When he asked us if our, speaking of white, babies were having babies? We just shook our heads. As much as we wanted to we could not help. We were as blind as he was. It wouldn't take long, just a few years, before this new perception of normal attracted the attention of the white babies.

Consider this: for the last two years, this being 2014, 40.7% of babies born in the US came from unmarried women. Should that be acceptable? I doubt if any of these girls, black or white or otherwise, ten, twenty, thirty, forty, or even fifty years after the fact, would say this option worked really well for them.

It is childish to pretend by 1969 the government did not know their grand scheme was flawed. It is inexcusable for the government not to stop. Take a time out. Rethink the plan. Try something different. By 1979 the thing Michele Obama likes to call a 'cultural shift' was readily apparent. By 1989 the deal was done. Now, 2014 has arrived. The American Black Family has been decimated, as is, our cultural understanding for the term, family. Two monkeys and a goat would fit the progressive understanding of what a "family" could look like.

*** [If you are under fifty you may not be able to recognize the destruction. You would have to be old enough to have witnessed both realities, lived within both 'constructions of normal', in order to see the change. This situation is a key element in social engineering. It is known the old ways die out because the people who practiced the old ways, die out. I once watched an interview with two elderly black scholars. I heard them speak to this issue. They remembered the black family had a lower divorce rate than the white family during the Great Depression. Then, they joked between themselves as to the reason. "We couldn't tell the difference!" And here's another view they possessed. They experienced being raised in a successful family. Not a rich one. Rather, one that produced emotionally healthy adults. And, they observed the new family normal; the one that doesn't produce emotionally healthy adults. These men had seen both realities.]

White and other ethic families are not far behind. Today, the latest statistics show 7 out of 10 black men will spend some time of their lives incarcerated. 7 out of 10 black women will have a baby outside of marriage. Books are being written to explain why marriage doesn't work for the black community anymore. Bigots like Jesse Jackson and Al Sharpton are consistently given television face time to blame white people. "White bigotry is the only cause for black folk problems".

Seven out of ten. Imagine Obama, Jesse, and Al looking over a group of 10 newborn black boy babies. It is inconceivable these men would not know the truth, the first cause, the fingerprints of misguided and failed government intervention, which has doomed these babies to what is most likely, a horrible life. By their actions the three of them are totally OK, perfectly fine, with seven of these black boy babies spending time in jail or prison. 7 out of 10 growing up believing the lies that got them there and the lies they learned while locked up. Life crushing lies. Prison time lies.

Obama, Jesse, and Al are equally OK with 7 out of 10 black girl babies growing up to be enslaved within the very visible walls of our welfare system. Stuck. Never being able to enjoy a life different from what they know. Obama, Jesse, and Al have got theirs. Their sons and daughters will be just fine. Obama, Jesse, and Al are rich. Their children and grandchildren are well cared for. They have great lives. They hang out with rock stars.

Lincoln and the Republicans got rid of slavery in America. President Johnson and the progressive democrats brought it back. Obama, Jesse and Al are laughing all the way to the bank. They got theirs. Their success came with a cost…the American Black Family.

"The people will decide for themselves what the truth is".

I once had a conversation with a recent school of Journalism graduate. His professor taught him to write the truth as he saw it and let the people decide for themselves what their version of truth will be. The following is my translation. "My professor said I have no responsibility for any consequence, intended or unintended, from the opinions I hold to be true. It's not my fault if a person adopts my views. There is no connection between me and my readers' future quality of life even though I went to school to gain the skills to effectively alter public thought. Even though I got into Journalism in the first place because I wanted to make the world a better place."

The American Education system is overly influenced by the arrogance of the progressive movement. They teach subject matter laced with lies. Purposely. Apparently, it is in their interest to avoid teaching journalism students an accurate understanding of how people learn, or any notion of civic responsibility. Also, it appears they teach teachers to spend as much time on their version of social 'improvement' as the curriculum they are being paid to teach.

Can you provide any other reason that would allow an 8 year old to be suspended for sexual harassment because he stole a kiss from a classmate on Valentines day? Do you think this boy would have been punished if the classmate he kissed were a boy? Another example. A child is told to cut out a picture from a magazine. His choice is a picture of a handgun. He is suspended for a week because he points the picture at a friend and says, "bang".

Today, most of a child's construction material to build their understanding of reality, to mimic, is based on 'logic' introjected from television. That boy did exactly what he had learned. The message of handguns and the way they are used is a thousand times more 'in their face' than the lonely one the school administrators use as punishment. Children are going to mimic the prevalent activities they observe and recognize as socially acceptable.

Parents should grasp this too. If you have unruly teenagers, the root for their behavior may very well lie in the confusion between the perfect world represented by the imagery of movies and television and the real world imagery associated with how they live. This is not a good time for being a parent and it isn't a good time to be a child. It would be great to be able to have one 'heart to heart' chat and make their 'thinking errors' go away. It just isn't that easy.

If the progressives are going to play doctor with our society, then someone needs to tell them to treat the disease, not the symptoms. If you are a non-progressive educator please stand up to the progressive elite. Right now we only see one flavor. Help us out. Let us know. Make public the distinction between their views and yours. One has to wonder, is coercion keeping you silent? Are teachers punished because they are not progressive?

This behavior by our educators and school administrators can only come from the progressive bag of ideological scat that falls under the heading, reality engineering. Congress fully understands the power of reality manipulation and you should too. You might be aware Congress recognized the wrong in the "Joe Camel" cigarette advertising that was being directed toward young people. They knew exactly how effective this type of ad campaign was and would be if allowed to continue. They had to know. They win elections using the same techniques.

It is bad to be a 'homophobe'.

Impossible! No person exists with that condition. True, it is bad and wrong to be disrespectful of any person. This term was invented as a label to shame people who in any way disagree with the total and complete acceptance of homosexuality within every arena of everyday life. Have you ever been around a person with a true phobia? A gut retching fear that overwhelms and super focuses the attention with only one aim, to put distance between them and the object of their fear. If you've seen it, you would remember it. Phobia is not a term to throw around lightly.

Can two distinct terms be joined to create a new word for our language. Yes. But, I don't have to agree with it. Myself, and I'm sure other people, perhaps you, do not have any fear of homosexual men. I exhibit no visible signs, internal or external, of a fear of gays or their behaviors. I suppose there are other people like me, who are offended by some homosexual behaviors.

When I see men swapping spit in public and fondling each other I am disgusted. So, for me, reality would be better served if I was labeled: homo-disgustant. I'm good with that. I should be allowed to embrace my feelings without condemnation.

I remember when I was hit on by a gay acquaintance. Again, I was not afraid. I was repulsed. So, in this case, call me a homo-repulsive.

I'm seeking to name my feelings honestly. Who gave anyone the permission to censor my thoughts? Freedom only remains pure if I'm allowed to embrace my feelings and thoughts. A persons actions and behaviors must be held to account before the law. Society requires it. However, our thoughts and feelings should be sacred. Check our Constitution. We have the right to personal thoughts and feelings and the right to express them so long as we do not harm others.

If a person claims hurt feelings because of my thoughts or speech then share that with me. We can discuss these things peacefully. Reasonable people can make room for each other. However, a simple assertion of hurt feelings should not have a greater claim to fairness over my right to my feelings and thoughts and my right to declare these feelings and thoughts peacefully and without malice.

Censorship is bad for America.

Certainly true according to everything I've ever heard or seen on television or classroom or any other venue. The whole premise of freedom of speech is rooted in the view there will be no censorship. Yet today, censorship is embraced in journalism and education, and progressive politics. We know it as "political correctness". It is the 'go to' tool to publicly shame any person or any opposing view that has found itself in the pubic eye.

'Political correctness' has become a type of social structure that was created by the progressives. It only has power if we as a people allow it. It can be made to go away. Just ignore it. Poke fun at the moron's who use it to influence how you think. You will be amazed!

Censorship is pure reality manipulation and it can also be nonverbal. Remember the Katy Couric Sarah Palin interview? From this she won the CBS Walter Cronkite award. From this she loss any hope of capturing the one demographic network news anchors need to keep their job; a majority of male viewers.

It was standard fare for Ms. Couric, when she decided to blindside Ms. Palin, with "the look". If you remember there was a commercial for the interview showing her being slightly behind Palin and walking up next to her. The viewer watched her form this god awful mean evil ugly facial expression. Palin was noticeably surprised and flustered.

The 'look' was meant to communicate to you and me NOBODY should like or approve of Sarah Palin. She intended to sway our opinion. I think it fair to say Katy Couric is very good at what she does. She communicated complete and total distain with that look. And, she was effective. But, she was too effective. Too many men had seen a very similar look being directed toward them. I would submit there are way too many men who have seen the exact same evil look of hatred and distain coming from an ex, or a soon to be ex. That look is used to convey this simple message: "Get out of my life, NOW!!"

The men who saw Couric do her 'look' thing received the message very, very, very clearly. And they did. They put distance between themselves and her. And, Ms. Couric's contract was not renewed.

A woman has a right to choose.

Yes, but at what cost? It is far easier to accept and defend the expression, "A woman's right to choose" than the more specific and accurate, "a mother's right to kill her baby". True? Still, the baby dies in either case. This progressive sponsored agenda is to frame their argument in socially acceptable language. A mother's right to kill her baby wouldn't work as well, would it?

We can see the whole social argument as a means to deflect from their true agenda. I think it is damage control to keep the cost down for all the women their policies have encouraged to get pregnant in the first place. This is how progressives solve the problems they create. Lie to you, hurt you, and destroy the evidence.

Democrats are for the working family.

NOT! If that were true America would be on her feet and working again. If that were the case hardly any working family would need government assistance. We could be at 96% employment if we were allowed to do the work to make the country energy independent. The progressive-democrat

34

agenda is best seen in what it is they are doing. Not in what they are saying!

Their goal appears to be to create a majority voting constituency comprised of people dependent in some fashion on government handouts. They must realize how hard it is to get a job!! They need dependent folks to vote for them. How else can one explain why they kept in place the social structures that continue to produce our current class of dependent American citizens? They excel with test tube results.

Life will be easy for the ruling class from here on out. They have the votes. But, at what cost? For almost fifty years far too many welfare babies have grown up to be welfare mothers with far too many of their sons growing up to be imprisoned. If Hitler had wanted this result he would have used the exact same methods. The outcome is totally predictable. No... Really... the outcome is totally predictable.

Retirement is a right.

Not really. The whole notion of working and being able to stop, when we are too old to produce effectively, is a new idea within the scope of human experience. It may be our normal now, but up until about 85 years ago, it wasn't. The progressives gave us social security. I'm thankful for it. Along with my union retirement I can get by. I'm probably luckier than most. I got in while it was still available.

Progressives acted on their belief the federal and state governments should set the retirement plan 'standard', raise the bar high, and for all American employers to provide a similar retirement plan. Work 30 years and retire with 50 to 60 percent of your base pay. Work 20 for the military and ten more for the Feds and you can double dip. Get two retirements. Become a world traveler. Live the life you deserve. Sounds nice to me. Except for the consequences.

Today a new term is being floated as if to help us become familiar with it. It is "unfunded liabilities". It means we have a re-occurring debt and no money to pay for it and NO plan to pay for it. Years ago, the progressives, the truly smart all knowing all seeing Americans, passed laws to make retirement available to Federal and State employees. Sounds good so far. The devil is in the details. Their retirement concept was a great idea except for one little flaw. They didn't submit a working plan to pay for it.

What we have inherited is a government sponsored Ponzi scheme. It works only for the first ones to get there. Here is where we are today. The Federal Government pension plan, as of 2011, is upside down 761.5 billion dollars. The States have a combined unfunded liability for their retirement plans which exceeds 452 billion dollars. Federal employees are way better off than their state counterparts. The federal government can print more money State governments cannot. If you want to get a grasp of just how much a billion dollars is try this. Count to one billion. The early numbers can be said in about one second. The larger numbers said quickly will take at least 5 seconds. Using this formula it has been estimated to count to one billion would take 127 years.

What this means to you is a billion dollars is a huge amount of money and right now city governments are beginning the process to default on their promise to pay retirement. State plans are not far behind. The money is not there. The whole retirement scenario turned out to be a delusion. This is bad for our firemen and policemen. It is bad for everyone. And, this disaster is not our fault. We trusted our leaders to do better.

The first cause of this shipwreck is the arrogant self-perceived

36

genius of the progressive 'I can make the world a better place' mindset. It gets worse. The unfunded liability for social security, Medicare, and Medicaid is 100 trillion dollars, and growing. One hundred thousand billion dollars, and growing. It has been calculated, as of today, there is only about 240 trillion dollars of total wealth on the entire planet. Could this be a problem? You think??

For forty years I've been hearing about the problem. Nothing was done to fix it. They just kicked the can down the road and with the help of TV news and commentary, scared Americans and blamed Bush, or some other anti-progressive. Today, for most people, it is a toss up if there will be ANY government service online when they retire. One has to wonder if it is not the goal of progressives to simply just eradicate America. We may not be able to escape this fate. Please Mr. and Ms. Progressive. No more help.

Obamacare is good for America.

Not! Everything the government touches turns stinky. History shows college was more affordable before government intervention. The cost of a home was less expensive before our government decided to help. Medical care was more affordable before Medicare and Medicaid.

I saw recently a man without insurance had a appendectomy and the hospital charged him 30 thousand dollars. Really? A one to two hour procedure? No wonder the Progressives' drool at the thought of being in control of healthcare. The same leadership is choking our oil delivery system to keep the cost artificially high. You think they would do better here? You think they would let this opportunity pass? With government intervention the cost of that procedure is likely to double. Do you really trust the government to stand between your Doctor and you? Do we really want to give them more ways to separate us from the little money we have? I don't think so.

There is no scandal in Benghazi.

"For more than a year, we have watched Republicans desperately and obsessively search for a scandal, which has not appeared. It is time to move forward," said Progressive Democrats Adam Smith and Niki Tsongas. A scandal which has not appeared? There is scandal on several levels. It is scandalous elected officials misrepresent the truth.

Also, there is scandal in the fact Americans have adapted to accepting 'political spin' instead of accurate representations of the facts. Spin is OK and lying is not? Really. If that is OK then how about, 'wage spin'? Are you willing to be OK if your promised wage is different than what you actually receive on your check? I don't think so.

And, there is scandal in the fact Americans were willfully mislead by ABC, NBC, and CBS news. For five days Susan Rice lied to American people, the United Nations, and the world. She, along with these news outlets, carried Obama's water. Without question nor conscience, they reported the event was due to a spontaneous eruption of violence predicated on an obscure internet video.

Fox News, during this time, reported the leaked real time and frantic messages from the Americans who died. The Progressive Hitler-like propaganda machine, ABC... NBC... CBS, proved beyond any question, beyond any shadow of a doubt, their true colors. The proof is in the pudding. They are not good for America and cannot be trusted.

Because ABC and NBC and CBS decided to mislead the American public, Obama was re-elected. The consequence of that deception is in both the Obamacare debacle and a

38

continued debased economy. Romney promised to build 20 nukes. That would have been a good start toward energy independence. He would have cleared the bench for practically all of Organized Labor. He would have put America back to work. It would be scandalous to NOT ignore ABC and NBC and CBS. Fool me once shame on you. Fool me twice shame on me. Fool me three times and my children suffer. We've been fooled for years.

There is scandal in the fact the Republicans fight like sissies. Benghazi gave Romney the opportunity to educate Americans, during the debates, to just how reality manipulation works and the role the press plays in creating the current delusions of reality. He did not go there. This is scandalous in the questions it raises. Are Republicans ignorant as to how we learn and acquire our version of reality? I find that hard to believe. The greater scandal is in the appearance our two party system has become a deception in itself. It appears Republicans are in agreement, behind closed doors, with the direction the Progressive Democrats want to take us. As, I said, they fight like sissies. I'm watching what they do, not what they say.

Ronald Reagan was right. The scariest thing a person can hear is: **"I'm with the government and I'm here to help."**

We have to call them something…

Had he not actually won the Nobel Peace Prize I may not have singled him out. To be nominated is one thing. To be selected is another. Obama won "for his extraordinary efforts to strengthen international diplomacy and cooperation between peoples." Mother Theresa took a lifetime. Martin Luther King gave his life. Obama did it all in his first eleven days in office. This doesn't pass the smell test.

I won't even attempt to offer any proof for the view I'm about to share. But, here is what I think happened. There was a meeting Obama attended with a person who could speak for the leaders of the Progressive movement. We may never know their names but for my purposes it isn't necessary. These would be very powerful people with the resources to launch a run for the presidency. Obama convinced them he was their guy.

If I'm wrong explain this. Not long after he won the senate seat in Illinois his picture graced the cover of Newsweek magazine. His image was painted to be the purple candidate. Neither blue nor red. A combination of the two. A superhero. The unique man who dwells above the fray. He was gifted by the gods with incredible wisdom and his only felt purpose in life is to bring people together. And he is willing, to give up all worldly pleasures, just for you.

Has there ever been a newly elected first term senator to be given this kind of roll out? His whole campaign was based on lies. Powerful lies made effective through reality manipulation. The Press served it up and spoon fed it to America. He was elected. America continued to be deceived and betrayed. Like sheep being led to slaughter, we re-elected him.

Obama cannot be separated from the progressive movement. Nor, would I suppose he would want too. However, the progressive agenda has proven itself to be disastrous for America and her people. If he did not act so arrogant, if he would have done something to fix the problems the progressive movement created rather than bring us new problems, I might have given him a pass.

No, he was elected because he chose to be the poster child for the progressive movement. He chose to follow their playbook and use deceit to gain the office, and with both houses held by the democrats he choose to use the power of the office to bring more enslaving legislation to our country. His face is our only true image for this kind of lunacy. For that, we will use it.

A new, never before recognized, level of national stupid is now apparent and Obama is the poster child. We will call the people who think they are smart enough to create a perfect world: the **Obama Class Moron**.

Who devised the plan to choke our gasoline delivery system by keeping the refineries operating at 95% capacity? **OCM's.**

Who wrote the legislation that made every American taxpayer a co-signer on home loans to people who were not prepared to purchase a home? **OCM's.**

Who decided it was best to borrow money we cannot repay to fund extended unemployment benefits rather than to put America back to work by building the infrastructure to make us energy independent? **OCM's.**

Who thinks it acceptable that 7 out of 10 black boy babies will spend time in jail or prison and not lift a finger to tell them why or effectively help them change their fate? **OCM's.**

Who thinks it acceptable that 7 out of 10 black girl babies will get pregnant and not be married continuing the pattern that is destroying the American Black Family? **OCM's.**

Who thinks it politically expedient to take advantage of the Black Family crisis and use the main stream media along with our schools and colleges to place all the blame on racist white people? **OCM's.**

What kind of educator, journalist or media outlet employee would align themselves with a philosophy that has a track

41

record of destroying peoples lives one person at a time? **OCM's.**

What kind of educator, journalist or media outlet employee would use the power of their position to publicly humiliate, via 'political correctness', another person for no other reason than their opposition to the progressive agenda? **OCM's**

What kind of person would convince a woman it is OK to kill her baby knowing they themselves won't feel any of the pain associated with the certain emotional trauma which follows? **OCM's.**

Who put into motion grand schemes of Utopian style living for all Americans and chose, to bankrupt the country over fixing the problem, which would have exposed their role in creating it? **OCM's.**

What kind of leaders would choose to create the conditions that cause our working class families to become dependent on government handouts as to create a voting block to insure they themselves could keep their jobs? **OCM's.**

Who are educating our teachers and school administrators with the belief they must use the classroom to help create a prescribed social reality without regard to the apparent negative consequences and even the possibility of future negative consequences? **OCM's.**

Who devised the plan to bring all health care in America under Federal Government control giving them the opportunity to jack the cost up like they did with gasoline? **OCM's.**

What kind of citizen would want a government that willfully deceives her people? **OCM's.**

What kind of citizen would trust ABC, NBC, or CBS news?
The Obama Class Moron.

We need to step up and we need to fix this mess. The Progressives' 'slavery through social engineering' agenda has insulted every American killed defending our freedom. They have insulted every American who has traded body parts so we can be free. The Progressive Democrats are too extreme and not good for America. They should be shunned.

In the meantime, we need to recover a thing that has been taken from us. We need to re-insert, back into public memory, the set of 'how to have a successful life' rules and tools. These rules and tools offer a better alternative to the Hollywood version that says, "You are supposed to be happy. Happiness is reserved for the prettiest, and the sexiest, and those who have the most money. If this is not you, then pretend, pretend, pretend.... Fake It... until you die or lose your job, or lose your family, or they cancel your credit cards, or you run out of drugs."

And, another thing we need to recover. Trust. As for the poor and the working class, we need to trust each other or we will die. We need to learn how to communicate, "I am not your enemy!" If we don't get it right, the species will move forward and we will be culled out, forgotten or worse. This is our heading, the course we are on, but it doesn't have to be.

The first step in recovering both, mutual trust within the poor and working class and the skill set necessary to enjoy a successful committed long-term relationship, begins with learning and factoring into our lives the internal species directives.

Chapter Three

The Internal Species Directives

a guide to recognizing and embracing our survival functions

In the early 1950's an over the counter drug, Thalidomide, was advertised to help ease morning sickness. Thousands of pregnant women took this drug. While helping the morning sickness as promised there was an awful unintended consequence. As these pregnancies came to term many babies were stillborn. A greater problem became evident. It is estimated up to seven thousand of these babies survived the womb yet were born with limb deformities. Some with no hands. Some with no feet. Some with no arms. Some with no legs.

Now let me give you an image you would do well to keep. I saw a documentary about one Thalidomide baby who at this time had a baby of her own. This woman was born with no arms, and yet possessed a powerful drive to be the best mother she could. My prominent memory is watching her change the baby's diaper using only legs and toes. Cloth diaper and safety pins. Incredible dexterity. Stunning. Amazing. Guaranteed to bring tears to your eyes.

Life with no arms was her Normal, her reality. I believe from what I saw she endured life below the poverty line. She was not well educated. She was not showered with gifts. No great travel opportunities. A local celebrity of sorts but not very many men lined up outside her door... if any. She did her best to get by. Her greatest joy came through the mother-child connection. That was enough. The one perfect thing she could treasure, drink in deeply, absorb completely. Just like any other mom. She had made it to the mountaintop. Not the moon. The mountaintop was enough.

Optimum Emotional Health

One of the messages prevalent in our culture is 'just a little bit more'. "Strive and reach hard to grasp that bit of pleasure which lies just beyond your fingertips." Just a little bit more money and you can be happy. The concept of continual happiness is presented as a must have for our new 'normal'.

We should not chase happiness. Never! Happiness, like everything else, is an illusion. You will never find the perfect world, that imaginary place which resides within a little section of your brain, to match your real world experience. Nothing is more elusive.

Our pursuit should be Optimum Emotional Health. This may sound dry but the opposite is true. The concept of Optimum Emotional Health rests on the premise, our species has built into the fabric of our being, a checklist of priorities, a 'must do' list in order for the species to survive.

It follows; to adhere to the checklist would result in a contented emotional field. To be out of sync with the checklist would result in a kind of 'species nagging' to tell us to get in line. This internal nagging would not escape the notice of the management feature of our sub-conscious mind, otherwise known as the Executive Decision Maker, a.k.a. EDM.

45

This is the common way anxiety works. It begins with two conflicting imperatives informing the EDM. In this case, it is the internal species directives telling the EDM to give attention to the survival checklist. At the same time, the EDM has another imperative it must follow, the existing cognitive structure, the developed 'how to do life' rules and tools. This 'double bind' creates the problem. The result is a feeling we know as anxiety.

This measurable and physical anomaly, this negative emotional field, can be, at best, just a tacit, below the surface, feeling that something is amiss. On the other end of the spectrum, it can be crippling… extremely debilitating. Here's the kicker. Sometimes we give our anxiety a name. Sometimes we mislabel and call it, 'not being happy'.

I believe this relates. In 2011 a report released by the Nation Center for Health Statistics showed the rate of antidepressant use in this country among teens and adults, age 12 and older, increased by almost 400% between the 1988-1994 data capture and the 2005-2008 data capture period.

23% of women between forty and sixty years old take antidepressants. Women are two and a half times more likely to take antidepressants than men. As I said, the common cause for anxiety is an internal battle between two compelling imperatives, creating the double bind.

As we look at our culture and compare that to the way most of us actually live, we can easily see the two most likely suspects. The internal species directives and the perfect world imagery provided by television.

It is thought women are more in tune with the species directives than men. Perhaps this is true. It certainly would explain the anxiety. Women evaluate their lives and some can just know "this" cannot be right. It doesn't help NOT to know WHY. Their personal explanation, the solutions offered up by the adult rational mind, cannot solve the problem. They deal with unhappiness when the real culprit is existential anxiety.

This is not a rational mind issue. It is an Executive Decision Maker issue. There also exists a conflict between our personal perfect world expectations, the one we adopted from the imagery our TV and Hollywood driven culture provided, and the real world we live in where we have to pay the bills and do the laundry.

Do I think the Progressive Reality Engineers know about this anxiety problem in our culture? Yes, I do. Have they offered a solution that addresses the first cause? No. They appear content to sit on the sidelines and watch America medicate the symptoms rather than treat the root.

Do I think the overall rise in recreational drug use correlates? Yes. Recreational drugs help people escape the pain associated with having to live in a very different world than the one their culture had taught them to expect.

An over medicated citizen is much easier to manipulate.

In the world before Progressive intervention, a child born into an emotionally healthy family would have had the EDM build into its rules and tools for doing life, the internal species directives. There would not, nor could not, be any conflict. Hence, a child raised in this environment would have normalized the feelings associated with emotional contentment. It is in this state of contented feelings we all should hope to live.

It is in this state, we can experience a deeper, and more stable sense, of happiness. Also, a child raised in this environment

47

would not buy into the perfect world, Hollywood driven culture, as completely or readily as a child not so fortunate. They would know a better alternative.

The Alpha Rules

We will call the internal species directives, the drives we must attend to in order for the species to survive, the Alpha Rules. When I was in the counseling program I became familiar with Maslows' Hierarchy of Needs. His ideas were presented in the shape of a pyramid. The top tier suggested the supreme drive would be 'self-actualization'. He lost me there. Seemed to 'artsy' for me. Just did not resonate.

Recently the pyramid was revised. Douglas Kenrick, a professor of psychology at Arizona State University and his team submitted a new understanding. Co-authored by Steven Neuberg, their research looked to interface psychology, biology, and anthropology with the goal to identify these critical internal species directives.

The new version 'leaped off the page' when I first read it. It spoke to me and I think they hit the proverbial nail right on the head. The first four rules are fundamentally the same. Their improvement is seen in the exchange from self-actualization to a more functional view informed from a species perspective. I will apply my blue collar language to these also.

Alpha Rule 1: We need a continual supply of food, clothing, and shelter.

Historically, our ancestors provided food for themselves through one or the combination of four methods. They would hunt for food. They would forage and gather from the local vegetation. They would plant seeds and harvest. Or, they would steal from someone else's stockpile.

They had to make their own clothing. It came from animal hides, or fabrics like wool, woven using the current technological understanding. Or, they stole clothing from someone else.

The common form of shelter was nature based as well. They would inhabit caves, or build dugouts, lean-to's, along with wood, mud, or stone structures. Or, they would steal a shelter already built by someone else.

There are a lot of thieves in our family tree…murderers as well. Survival of the fittest became an art form. One clan of people would unite to stockpile food, make clothing, and build shelters knowing another clan was out there that would try to steal and even kill them to get all they had worked for.

The social environment has changed but the species directive has not. You need a continual supply of food, clothing, and shelter. You would be wise to recognize there are people, powerful or otherwise, out there that will steal it from you.

The greatest stealing weapon of all time has been the ink pen. We have laws on the books that make it legal to steal. Yes, the people we elected did that to us. Social structure has been developed to make the stealing feel like 'normal'. We live with this but it doesn't have to be this way.

Sometimes, when we are up to our armpits in alligators, we cannot spare looking away from our immediate problem, to recognize the full array of danger within the swamp.

Now for the really bad news, it comes in two flavors. First, focus on the concept of a 'civilization'. It is a super expanded version of the early clan. A civilization forms when clans unite with the purpose of mutual protection from murderers and thieves. Customs and laws had to be developed because they understood murderers and thieves do not make good neighbors. The customs and laws initially focused on protecting food, clothing, and shelter ownership.

Civilizations come and go. Sometimes a powerful outside invader breaches the border and takes over. A new civilization is formed. Much of the time, the dying civilization will simply implode, collapse upon itself. This always happens for a reason.

The first and unifying reason for its existence, "no murderers and thieves allowed", will have become forgotten, a thing erased from public memory. A new normal will emerge. Like a social virus people will once again steal from each other, legally, corporately, or otherwise. Public trust, that cohesive force which binds a people together, will degrade. Eventually, it will disappear. Not long after that, the civilization becomes like a carefully constructed line of dominoes. And, finally one tips over. Historically, a new civilization, with values and purpose similar to the original, will rise 'out of the ashes' and start afresh.

Today, the dominoes are in position. Consider the natural consequence to our world once the first domino falls. Almost every American living today does not have the skills to survive 'in the wild'. We have not been trained to be a hunter, gatherer, or a farmer. For the most part these, and other valuable old time survival skills, have been erased from public memory.

Even if we were so trained, the wilderness conditions and availability are not sufficient to support the current population. I suppose an alternative would be, we could all revert back to using option number four, the stealing and murdering option. This one is sure to be on the table.

Once the first domino falls, it won't be long, before the food supply line is affected. We live in an extremely complex society. The food you ate last night had many stops before it found its way into your refrigerator. You can track these stops with a flow chart. You block one stop. Just one stop. And that particular food cannot get to your house.

Fault nor cause will not be your concern once the food supply line fails. Be aware of this. No city in America has more than a seven-day supply of food on its grocery store shelves at any one time. Most people do not have more than a week's supply of groceries in their home. Consider the potential consequences to you and your family.

Should the supply line breakdown last only a week or two, your family will most likely survive. If it is longer, the odds become dismal. There is another feature about our species which none of us, in our fat and happy condition, can understand or even care to discuss. Humans sometimes will eat other humans. In this scenario, we all become a potential food source.

My focus is to inform the poor and blue collar working class family. The rich people have options you and I don't. Right now, across our nation, there are compounds being constructed to store food and clothing and to provide safety and shelter to weather this upcoming storm. For these people, it is no longer an "if", it has become a "when". They are buying into these compounds now because the "when" has become an 'in my lifetime' kind of 'when'. Perhaps, you and I should think like them.

As I observe the social and cultural landscape I see what looks like our Progressive government deliberately inciting racial tension. Why? When this event happens, their plan is for the poor and working class families to wage war against each other. They are telling us who our enemy is and who we need to kill. They want us to be the first to die. This will give them an opportunity to form a new civilization, to their liking, out of our collective ashes.

Alpha Rule 2: We need to feel safe and secure.

In a perfect world there would be no fear. Short of that, we need to have at least one place to go where we do not have to be afraid. Without such a place anxiety will almost certainly develop. Typically the fear free zone should be our home. The Hebrew greeting "Shalom" works here. We translate it as 'peace' but it carries a deeper meaning than the absence of war. It conveys the image of the ultimate social and cognitive safe place, a place without enemies. A place where we can rest and enjoy our family undistracted by fear.

For optimum emotional health, your home should and must become your sanctuary. Your first and last 'fight' should be to ensure your home is your "Shalom", your family safe place. And, you should reserve the right, to use any and all measures, to protect your sanctuary. This was written into your genes, it is deep within your code, you were born with this directive, and you would do well to trust its wisdom.

Alpha Rule 3: We need friendly social connections.

We came into this world anticipating, that is, believing and expecting, everyone will like us and treat us with dignity and respect. Of course each of us arrived egocentric. When boiled down, egocentric will ultimately be expressed as, 'me first'. A strange paradox exists between the loving, accepting environment we, at our core, are seeking and anticipating, and the very different reality we have learned to accept. The foundation for all our world religions are based on their explanation and understanding of THE answer to this dilemma.

Here is what you have proven within your personal life experience. We are all drawn to safe, loving, social acceptance… period. We will settle for safe and socially accepting affiliations. Sometimes, socially accepting is the best we can find. Life has taught us not everything we once believed to be safe, loving, and accepting turned out that way.

Children in our culture are plagued with trust issues before they get into the first grade. The EDM is designed to work best within a truthful environment. It struggles to make sense out of anything else. This is our world. "Relationships fail because trust issues prevail."

I'm describing the 'adapting factor'. Not all that long ago, in our society, there were common, unwritten, socially validating, and re-enforcing 'how to do relationship' rules. The once customary, please and thank you, has been replaced with "no problem". It is more normal for the public to show aggression and disrespect rather than courteous and mutually respectful behavior. If you took the time, you could develop your own list. Find an old person and ask them how it once was. Learn for yourself the ongoing social change.

Alpha Rule 4: We need to feel significant.

This need is related to the previous one. The former need told us to be social. This need tells us we must be competent in our social endeavors. It also tells us our goal is recognition, approval, acceptance… respect.

At its core, this need tells us we like to be recognized. Not always the 'receiving an award' kind of recognition; no, a simple greeting from a friend or stranger works just fine. Eye contact, even better with a smile, which says, I see you. I know you exist. You are OK with me.

But, there is another side. This 'need to feel significant' does not communicate itself very well. 'Approximately' appears to be good enough. A range of behaviors from self-serving to altruistic, appear to scratch its itch. It's almost like the internal species directive is speaking a language the EDM cannot fully comprehend.

It appears we search for an undefined source of approval. We never arrive. Sometimes we feel close, only later to realize 'not quite'. Eventually, the feeling fades. Then reappears. This pursuit drives our creative side. It also causes us to believe there is a place, perhaps just over the next hill, which will provide, if not the answer, at least the correct question to ask. This drive propels our species. And, as such, it propels you. However, it does not tell us if we are moving forward, or backward, or in a circle… a potential problem for all of us.

Alpha Rule 5: We need to qualify, and then select, a life partner.

The internal species directives are the rules for species survival. The continuity of our species existence requires making babies. However, producing babies cannot be seen as an end in itself. Human babies do not immediately stand up and join the herd. Human babies need to be nurtured. When we look at our lifespan, we average 15 to 20 per cent of our lifetime in the being nurtured phase.

It should be understood, to properly nurture a baby, it is necessary to have a steady supply of food, clothing and shelter. This is not an option. Historically, the ability to provide these life-sustaining elements, was the normal and accepted criteria that had to be met, before a man would begin the 'mate acquisition' process. When I was 16, my great grandmothers' old neighbor and friend, who had watched me grow up, saw me visiting and came over to speak. She offered this advice. "Ricky, make sure you build your pen before you buy your pigs." That's all she said. She then turned and walked away. I was a city boy and had already adopted a different perspective. I can tell you I had two children before I truly understood all the wisdom in her words. She was painfully accurate!

Historically, women played the feature role in nurturing children. The man was to be the breadwinner. It has only been in the last fifty years or so since these roles began to fade away. The shift began just about the time television was common in the home. Now, the current understanding of family 'normal' looks nothing like this. My children are grown and have families of their own. So, believe me, I get it. I know the way it was, is nothing like the way it is, today. However, that doesn't mean it is the best way.

It is really helpful to look at this 'image of family' transition as a 'social experiment'. Government intervention needs to be considered. They've effectively changed the rules. Men are now optional. Men appear as only necessary to make the baby and pay child support. The government will do the rest. It is the government that has rewritten the social rules. And, I ask you to look around. How is this experiment working?

The species is not going to change the way it survives based on government intervention.

This government intervention experiment will fail and prove the failure in everyone's life that practices it. The misery index in America is very high right now and our government's fingerprints are all over it. Again, thanks to the progressive genius and their wild imaginations.

I'll make a brief case for the old way. Because the human baby is a social creature, its introduction to society, its first social environment is the family. The family is the species preferred nurturing vehicle to help the baby acclimate to the world it recently entered. Historically, the family begins with one man and one woman. Men are the breadwinner. Women are the chief nurturer. Don't allow television fantasy to be your model for a successful life. The species survival rules work much much better.

Adapt your life to the species model and don't waste time chasing the now socially accepted delusions. It has been observed, "the poor will always be with us". There is no shame in being poor. I know it is hard to imagine living on one income. The price of housing is so expensive. However, remember this, there is no guarantee the culture we know as normal today will remain so throughout your life. You may be alive during the collapse. The Hollywood success model will vanish overnight. What I'm saying is to explore your options. A better way waits to be discovered. The closer you get to 'living off the land' will work better for you and your family in the long run.

Try to keep this thought in front of you. The best way to do family should be your life pursuit. If we remember that every life can be seen as an experiment, then it follows, if the species had thought there was a better format to raise a child and do family, it would have come up with it. We've had forty thousand years to experiment. Alternate formats can work. They are just not the 'best' as the species defines 'best'.

Here's what all this means to you. For men, do not get into a relationship unless you are ready, willing, and able to provide a continual supply of food, clothing and shelter. You are also to be the chief protector for your family. Be prepared for that. You don't want a steak knife in your hand when the men breaking down your door have guns.

Women, don't get into the relationship unless that man has proven to you, and maybe even to your parents, that he is ready, willing, and able to make that commitment. Good intentions and promises do not apply. Hooking up may feel OK, but remember, that voice comes from your Executive Decision Maker who learned from watching television and going to the movies. The EDM 'proved' the accuracy of this view by watching your friends and by your mutual perceptions of social normal. This is a classic thinking error. Let your Adult Rational Mind make this important decision for you.

And, don't get into the relationship unless you are willing to be the chief nurturer for your babies. If you are expecting a Hollywood lifestyle and this man you are with is not a successful Hollywood actor, then you are lying to yourself. Don't go there. Stay real. And, don't even allow yourself to consider the Bridezilla model. That is social failure 101.

As pretty as you are today remember it will not last, it is extremely temporary. "Beauty is only skin deep." Another old expression lost from public perception. Shallow and hollow people seek to measure their worth by sexual attractiveness. I know this is our 'normal'. However, a lifetime can be wasted thinking this way. It is a dead end. Another thing to unlearn before you can achieve optimum emotional health.

Check it out for yourself. Remember, everybody is a social experiment as is every generation. My generation saw both realities and was morphed into the change. This cultural shift made the headlines and was identified as the 'sexual revolution'. If you want to witness for yourself the survivors of the sexual revolution just go to where lonely old men and lonely old women hang out. You will find plenty of them there.

Unrealistic expectations are the recipe for disappointment. True for me. True for you.

Alpha Rule 6: We need to keep the mate we have.

Today, progressive thinking seems to ask, "why a life partner"? "Why not a series of ten year partners?" "Why not something else?" Just the fact we can ask these questions prove we are in the middle of a grand social experiment. If you are one of the many who have been in and out of quasi-permanent relationships, you might ask yourself a different question, "How has that worked for me?"

I'm one of you in that regard and I can report, "not so well". I'm old enough to have been in the company of older couples who were on the backside of enjoying a successful, long term, committed relationship. Some even revealed a very important and key detail. As one man expressed, "I've only had sex with one woman and I believe she's had sex with only one man." From where I stand, I would say, "they won".

A human baby cannot enjoy a stable, loving, family environment if the star players are switched like it's a hockey game. This may be our new cultural 'normal' but it doesn't mean it ought to be this way. Imagine what the baby is doing with this kind of definition for family? At a minimum it is saying… this is normal. Sadly, the consequence for this sense of family normal is almost destined to produce an excessive amount of discontented and anxiety riddled living. Now look at what can be expected to follow, the relationship garbage the child adopts as normal will be passed onto its' children. Don't let this happen. You don't want that guilt.

This species directive 'to keep the mate we have' creates a problem for people today. The skill set, the proven relationship rules and tools for enjoying a successful long term committed relationship, are being erased from public memory. What this means is, if it was your desire to live within the boundaries of a successful committed long term relationship, you might not know how to bring it about.

If you are among the majority who carry flawed relationship rules and tools, this will not necessarily exclude you from reaching this goal. However, it does mean you will have to 'unlearn' your existing flawed relationship rules and tools and replace them with the proven successful set.

Alpha Rule 7: We need to be effective parents.

Effective parenting, as far as the internal species directives are concerned, has little to do with soccer games or piano practice or lots of toys underneath the Christmas tree. It certainly doesn't mean having the ability to give your daughter super white teeth or breast augmentation. It cannot mean providing your children with expensive clothes, cell phones, gameboys, and the like, just because you feel good doing it.

Effective parenting, as far as the internal species directives are concerned, is far simpler. You need to show your children, how to build a life, using the internal species directives as their guide. Show them the need, the energy, the preparation, the focus and commitment necessary to maintain a continual supply of food, clothing and shelter.

Create a safe and secure environment for your children to experience. Make your home their sanctuary too. Reinforce the special status of the fear-free zone and proclaim its value. Acknowledge loving behaviors. Lovingly rebuke those behaviors, which are not so loving. Model what it looks like to enjoy each other.

Marvel over your children. Cause them to feel the family

connection. Help them to see their special value. Help them to choose their social connections wisely. And, be there for them as they are sure to discover, not all of their choices turn out well. Guide them toward the adventure awaiting them as they begin the process to build their own life.

Help them to understand the species perspective and the historical value it gives to the Family. Teach them it is best to have just one life partner. In our culture, this is certain to sound odd, but that in itself does not make it wrong. Perhaps, the most significant element in the concept of building a life, is selecting a partner to do it with. Life works best as a team sport. Be their example.

Show your children how to sanctify, to make holy, the relationship you enjoy with your life partner. Help them to understand the relationship rules and tools, which are prevalent in our culture, did not escape their notice. Most likely, they adopted some rules and tools which look a lot like thinking errors. Prepare them for the need to recognize unsuccessful behaviors and how to adjust, unlearn, and adopt a better set. Show them a lifestyle worth mimicking.

Then, turn them loose. They will know, as an emotionally healthy adult, it is now their job to repeat the process.

Chapter Four

The Alpha Man

allow me to introduce you to a friend of mine

I would not be so arrogant as to presume 'my' wisdom is a thing worthy for the good of all humankind. I'm not that smart. Not even close! But, I know someone who is.

Let me introduce you, to the Jesus, most Christians do not know. I can say that because I went to college to learn about Jesus and to become a Pastor. Was I ever surprised!

Quite possibly, the Prop 16 thing may be starting to ramp up. Hear me out please. One thing I learned is that Christianity is much more than just adhering to the teachings of Jesus. Christianity, like Islam and Judaism, is best studied as a theological construction. Like our constitution, over the years certain 'amendments' and 'clarifications' have been added.

Not everyone agreed with another groups choice of an 'amendment' or their 'clarification'. History shows a new group would form based on their preferred understanding known as their, 'doctrinal distinctive'. If that were not true we would not have over 2,000 forms of Christianity here in the United States today. One way to view the current state of the Christianity is to think of it as excessively egocentric.

61

Lost in the wash is the historical Jesus and his message. Not the one we hear every Christmas and Easter. Not the one diluted through the prism of theological craftsmanship. Not those. We need to hear the other one. His version. His words. His directives. He came to teach a greater possibility. We need to hear it. We can know the full essence of what it means to be human. We can have a better life experience without changing jobs. And, this is not a thing we have to purchase. It is free.

I'm not here to denigrate Christianity. I'm here to make public the relationship teachings and behaviors which would qualify Jesus to be a 'preventive therapist'... on a worldwide scale. I'm here to communicate to you the things he thought to be crucial for you to know.

Jesus can be seen from multiple perspectives, but for the purpose of this discussion, we will look at Jesus as the world's first reality engineer. More so, he was the world's first relationship engineer. He intended to change the way people thought and how they practiced their relationships. And, not only for the people who were alive then, but also for everyone who would live after he was gone.

As to who Jesus actually was, you do not have to think like me. I'm old school. I believe Jesus came into our world as an agent of change and sent here by the omnipotent, omnipresent, omniscient creator of the universe. But you don't have to believe that in order to benefit from his teachings.

Jesus could be seen as your version of an ancient astronaut. A space cowboy who stopped by to help. Perhaps, a cosmic therapist who understood our design and came to present a 'patch' to help us overcome a serious design flaw. Who could argue Jesus was not an extra-terrestrial? He certainly did not come from around here. I think you will find, it was more important to Jesus, for you to accurately know what he said, than to accurately know who he was.

In order for you to hear effectively my intended message we need to construct a mutually understood framework of definitions, terms, and concepts. We're going to add another wing to your reality structure. Otherwise, we might just talk past each other. I think you will find this interesting.

The Jesus Perspective

Lordship

We will try to discover Jesus' phenomenology, his unique perspective. Lordship, in this case, is your commitment to allow Jesus to be your relationship instructor. Lordship, to him, would never be used as a intimidation device. **It is a therapeutic structure.** The concept of lordship provides a 'work-around' for the two major conflict producing issues associated with developing relationships, the trust and intimacy issue and the egocentric me first issue.

Here is the model. When two people decide to form a relationship they invariably bring with them certain types of relationship garbage. At the top of the list would be trust issues and the egocentric based relationship rules and tools learned from our culture. Lordship says to each relationship partner, "your way may work for you but my way will work for both of you". From another angle he sets the tone, 'it's my way or the high way'. 'You'll do it my way or it won't work at all.' In principle, lordship is like a learning contract between Jesus and the student. It might be helpful to know, in the original language, 'follower' also translates as student or apprentice.

Within the Lordship relationship model, each relationship

63

partner is to have an individual learning agreement with the teacher. "Jesus will teach, I will learn." Basically, this is not a 'couples' contract. Rather, its success depends on the individual, forgoing their own socially corrupted version of relationship 'normal', and adopting his.

A de facto kind of contract will emerge between the two relationship partners. They each, as individuals, agree to mimic his relationship model. The superior contract is between the individual and the teacher. The de facto contract will develop between the two relationship partners, and that will communicate, each is to learn these new rules and tools, both individually and together. The outcome is predictable. Because, they will be using the same relationship playbook, it will make it easier to stay on the same relationship page.

Should a disagreement arise, the playbook will be the referee. Not the husband. Not the wife. The instructions. While the instructions do not address 'how' to get through every possible life issue, his model will guide the relationship in the midst of these 'storms'.

A new platform is created for overcoming the 'me first' impulse and for developing mutual trust and intimacy.

Repent

Jesus began his teaching career flying solo, a single voice. He did have a roll out of sorts. But, it was nothing like Obamas' roll out. Another man, in the spirit of the Old Testament prophet, let the people know he was coming. They both used the same expression to catch the people's attention. Repent!

Repent is a common term in church circles. Too bad for us we were taught the 'theological' definition rather than what the people actually heard. The theological shortcut provided is to mean, stop sinning, 'turn away' from sin. But, this cannot be what the people actually heard.

Understand, the recorded original language was not the more technical and specific classic Greek. These events occurred in Judea, not Greece. The Greek spoken was different. It was the language of the working class; the 'business language' of the civilized world.

When John and later Jesus were heard shouting, 'Repent!', the people heard something different than 'turn away'. The classic Greek understanding would mean, to 'expand your mind'. The common folk version was most likely communicated, 'learn something new'. The actual understanding may have been heard as, 'check this out!' I'm going with 'learn something new'.

Miracles, Signs, and Wonders

The miracles were Jesus' rollout. Jesus was born into a blue collar working class family. He was known for most of his life just as the son of a carpenter. His family did not have wealth or status. He did not grow up on the fast track for success. He was not socially well connected. He was blue collar... like us. And, he came to talk... to people like us.

The secular historical records of the day reveal the Palestinian world knew about Jesus in his lifetime. He was not "invented" hundreds of years later. Something happened, in his lifetime, to make him famous. There had to be a 'first cause,' which enabled him to capture the attention of his world... in his lifetime.

Two thousand years later, the only plausible explanation would be the miracles actually happened. In that day and age, without the benefit of a Hitler like propaganda machine, without any public 'message injection system' technology, fame and public awareness could only spread by word of mouth.

Eye witnesses telling one other person. One person telling a group of people. A group of people telling one person. Jesus, at the end of his life, was a public celebrity. The reason? It was the miracles.

Jesus used the miracles to validate the importance and the authority of his message.

Blind, Lost, Enslaved

A key component of Jesus' message is the view, everyone in our species, all of us, has a defect of sorts. He never gave this defect a specific name other than Sin. This term fit the culture of the day and he communicated his message within the context of the local religious culture. Keep that in mind.

This is why I think Jesus to be, among other things, a reality engineer. He recognized the folks were living one type of lifestyle unaware there was a better one available. They just couldn't see it. Their adopted rules and tools, absorbed from the local culture, became their 'normal'. And, as such, there was no reason to reevaluate.

Jesus used "being enslaved", "being lost", "being blind" language to communicate to his audience; they are not able to know what they lacked. Today, psychologists acknowledge, even more than a prison cell, there is nothing more enslaving than the normalized belief system, a persons' set of rules and tools for doing life.

Jesus knew we came into this world blind. We didn't arrive with a glossary or approved set of definitions to make sense out of our world. We relied on the existing culture to 'take us by the arm' and lead us throughout our living experience. We arrived fully dependent on other people and very willing to let their beliefs and opinions guide us.

In a real sense, Jesus is telling us to embrace our blindness. Embrace our lost-ness. Embrace the fact we are enslaved within our existing and culturally driven rules and tools for doing life. It is from this perspective we are better able to recognize our need to move forward... to learn something new.

You must be born again

Science gives us a new perspective to revisit positions taken within a theological context. There is a foundational Christian understanding associated with this expression, "born again". And, I cannot agree with it anymore. Here's the background.

One night a bewildered and elderly Pharisee came to visit. If it were today, he might be an old school, fire-breathing fundamentalist, who believed he and his group were the only true believers. Had it not been for the miracles he never would have given Jesus the time of day. But, because of the miracles, this man came with questions.

Nicodemus was confused and couldn't make sense out of this strange mans' preaching. Jesus responded by telling him he would need to be born again. I believe he was referring to the first birth; that moment in time when we became aware. When the consciousness came online and began to absorb its rules and tools for doing life from the existing culture.

Ergo, the problem. The things Jesus felt to be important, were way different than what this old man, had lived his entire life believing. The rules and tools he trusted, those he had adopted from his father and grandfather and culture, did not match Jesus' message.

Let's review the quote, "I tell you the truth, no one can see the kingdom of God unless he is born again." Now, my blue collar understanding. Jesus is telling this man, you cannot get it, and you will never be able to understand with your current rules and tools. "Your existing computer program was written with faulty information. There is no way to communicate successfully between your existing code and the new one I'm attempting to install."

"My message would make perfect sense if you were born and raised within the Kingdom of God environment. But, you weren't and therefore we might as well be speaking different languages. If you really want to understand, then, you will need to unlearn the old system and replace it with the new information I'm providing."

The orthodox theological understanding of the 'born again experience' includes a 'felt awareness' of a new beginning. It is often referred as a 'crisis experience'. This experience is explained as God's Spirit coming to dwell within you, meshing his Spirit with your spirit. Most of the time this happens when people are given a choice within an emotionally charged preaching event. Live the old way that is not working or accept the promises associated with a better way now being offered. When people choose the better way, it is expected they will feel something happen inside, which provides evidence for the event. The Christian understanding if given and the EDM accepts the definition without question. For me, what was felt was the discovery phenomenon. It was the 'Ah Ha' or the 'moment of clarity' event when the EDM decided the new way to live is better than the old way and made the internal rules and tools change.

Kingdom of God

It is important to note, the only reason Jesus came, by his own admission, was to make known the Kingdom of God. He didn't have a list of many reasons, with this one being the most important. To make known the Kingdom of God is THE reason. Everything else, all other theological premises and understandings, should be subservient to this and this alone.
If we're going to make a theological construction about Jesus, then it follows; we should let him tell us where to begin.

Jesus, in response to questions and confusion, provided many different images and analogies, as he tried to explain to us 'earthlings' what the environment he called, the Kingdom of God, looks like. Some of the images indicate a kind of location to house our existence after we die.

Another image explains how the Kingdom of God would expand within this world. I really like this one. It shows the understanding we know today as systems theory. He uses a making bread analogy. 'Like yeast working its way throughout the dough.' Influence and outcome. This was his plan to get his message out: One person influencing those around him, and they in turn influencing others.

In another place we can find, and this will be our focus, the Kingdom of God exists within a relationship environment, which comes into being, when the relationship partners practice Lordship along with his 'how to do relationships' teachings. I call this place, Alphapeace, the ultimate emotional safe place.

One thing he makes very clear. Choice. He tells his audience they have a choice. They can take the broad path to destruction. Keep your existing rules and tools. Or, take the narrow path, and discover a better way to do life. No arm twisting. Choose door number one or door number two.

The Communication Dilemma

Try to imagine what it would have been like to be him. In his mind he has an image of a more effective relationship lifestyle and his only way to communicate is to use the language and the culture of the day. I'm sure he could 'tell it' better than the people could 'hear it'. This is part of the problem. We are left today with the recorded memories of what the first students heard.

Verbal communication works well enough when people are familiar with each other and talking about ideas and concepts they share. Non-verbal gesturing and expression helps to connect the dots. As we all know, sometimes we don't feel like we've been heard. Every one of us would prefer to have a sense of confidence the other person heard our intended message accurately.

Accurate and effective communication of any message in never a slam dunk. To assume the listener heard you accurately, just because you said it, is kind of arrogant, don't you think? Sometimes accuracy is not so important. Just interacting together is enough. Other times, clarity and clear messaging is very important. In those times, both persons should plan their words and behaviors to ensure the desired result.

Some forms of communication are strictly behavioral and transmitted visually. I haven't heard this expression in a long time. Years ago it seemed to be popular. "Do what I say, not what I do." My dad said it. And I've heard other dad's say it. I think I remember saying it myself. I marvel, now, just how dumb this parental instruction really is.

The stronger, more influential message, as it relates to adopting a behavior, will always be the 'what I see you doing'. That's how we were designed. The example I used in a previous section works here. The boy who cut out a picture of a handgun, and was suspended for a week, because he pointed the picture at a classmate and said," bang", explains this design feature very well.

His culture, via television and video games, taught him this is what a person is supposed to do with handguns. He's seen that message a thousand times more than the one our school administrators are trying to instill. The lesson here to learn is, teachers must give better attention to the way our species 'learning mechanism' operates. If not, they will waste a lot of energy and create problems, which challenge the abilities of the child's rational mind, as well as the parents. Perhaps, we would do better if we recognized there are two 'American Education Systems'. One is found in our schools and curriculum. The more effective and influential American Education System can be seen in television and program content.

Jesus did not place any stock in the 'do as I say, not what I do' teaching methodology. He understood our species. He incorporated the modeling and introjection methods into his communication plan. He knew the relationship behaviors a child sees will be the ones it mimics.

Consider what was important to him. Jesus did not leave his students with a whole list of final instructions. He didn't. He just had two. One said, "to go into all the ethic groups and make students". The other said to "teach them to observe all I have commanded you."

Within the 'commands' was the core teaching principle. Mimic these behaviors. He provided verbal imagery and his style of living mirrored the behaviors included within the imagery. He taught his students by example. They in turn were to be examples to their families and friends. They were to be the 'salt' and 'light'.

Let's see how it worked for him. The Book of Acts describes itself as the history of the early church, the first 25 years or so. We can see information in it to suggest Jesus' "way" was implemented and successfully practiced. The term "Christian" is first seen here. It was not meant to be complimentary. It was used to label and ridicule.

That select group of early followers had a noticeably different approach to living. They were content with their lives. Meanwhile, their neighbors could not comprehend how the poor and blue collar working class, along with the slave class, could find contentment considering their station and circumstance. So, many of their neighbors ridiculed them and dismissed them as foolish.

But, not all of them. What started out in a small and wayward section of the Roman Empire would eventually spread and cover it completely. It took three hundred years. And, it also took the lifestyle form of communication practiced by the poor and blue collar working class, along with the slave class, to make it happen. Three hundred years of children raised in the Alphapeace environment. Modeling and Introjection 101.

The rich and the powerful were not so affected. Go figure. "Check this out!" The secular historians of the day recorded the most visible distinction between the Christians and those who were not. The Christians practiced loving behaviors.

Jesus' methodology worked. If we looked at this as a social experiment, even todays atheist would agree it was a complete, over the top, success. Then, the wheels began to fall off.

Around the same time the blue collar working class were living the 'Jesus lifestyle' and causing the positive social consequence, the Christian teachers and institutional leaders were in the process of creating a formal religious structure, along with the 'approved' written belief system. The consequence of their 'human thinking' intervention, would not only break the social change momentum, it would forever prevent it from reoccurring.

Consider these references from my college textbook, Church History In Plain Language, by Bruce L. Shelley. Here's the context. Emperor Julian (332-63) wished for his empire to return to the old religion. He couldn't get much traction. Out of frustration, Julian offered these thoughts:

"Atheism (Christianity) has been specially advanced through the loving service rendered to strangers, and through their care for the burial of the dead. It is a scandal that there is not a single Jew who is a beggar, and that the godless Galileans care not only for their own poor but for ours as well; while those who belong to us look in vain for the help that we should render them." (P. 36) "Not a single Jew who is a beggar." A nice testimony, don't you think?

Now, let's explore some behaviors the established Christian leadership thought proper and permissible. The issue at hand was the need to make orthodox a single view of the nature of Jesus. Dr. Shelley took time to expose the dark political side, the politics of personal destruction, which occurred. False charges, lies, and slander caused Nestorius, a proven leader with a large following, to be exiled from Rome. Shelley says his views were not heretical, most likely he was a victim of misunderstanding and misrepresentations. Wow!

73

Another quote gives us a clearer picture. "The whole affair was disgustingly riddled with power politics. American church historian Williston Walker called it 'one of the most repulsive contests in church history.'" We are also told when the Pope's entourage arrived they approved and endorsed the action. (P.113)

One more quote that provides a snapshot of the practiced blue collar faith in action. "Athenagoras, a Christian philosopher at Athens, put it this way, 'Among us are uneducated folk, artisans, and old women who are utterly unable to describe the value of our doctrines in words, but attest them by their deeds'". (P. 73)

An old axiom tells it plainly. "Those who can… do and those who cannot… teach." Between the two, who do you think Jesus would approve? The poor and blue collar working class families who practiced his teachings or the educated, socially elite, creators and teachers of institutional orthodoxy?

Today, you and I do not have the ability, not even the imagination, to accurately assess the damage these early leaders of the church did to our lives.

Nobody escaped this consequence. This world we all suffer is our 'normal'. The life you are living is not Gods' plan. We had a chance. It was working. But, the arrogance of our 'betters' took it away from us. Another example of good intentions with horrible consequences. "I think therefore I'm right". This goes way past believing in the 'inspiration of scripture'. This asks us to believe in the 'inspiration of theological decisions'. I can't do that. There is no way the Creator of the Universe could be that dumb.

Did anyone else hear Jesus say, "All authority on heaven and earth has been give to me"? Why supersede his authority?

Jesus also asked, "Why call me Lord, and not do what I say?" And, "Why do you disobey God for the sake of your traditions?" Good questions don't you think? Jesus also defined what his students will look like. "If you practice my teachings, then you will be my student, then you will know the truth, and then the truth will set you free." He never mentions the need to learn doctrine. We think it is important. Maybe this is where we got it wrong.

Look at what the Church says it believes and look at what it does. Compare that to what Jesus said to do. Simple systems theory. Whatever is happening right now in the system, the system is perfectly designed to produce that result. If you want to prove or destroy a really good religious paradigm, use systems theory.

If I've got your Prop 16 running at full gear, don't do like that other religion does. Don't feel like you have to defend your God. The God of Abraham, as I believe him to be, is an all powerful God. He doesn't need man, a puny creature at best, to defend him. If God has a beef with me, let him deal with me. He put me in this world. He can take me out.

By the way, have you ever asked yourself, what kind of God would need a man to defend him?

Defend, instead your religious paradigm. Not to me. Rather, defend it to yourself. If your belief system meets your needs then keep it. If you've bought into all the excuses given for the sexual predators, the high Christian divorce rate, and all the other stuff, then keep what you have. If you believe Jesus told us to do things that cannot be done, keep what you have. Or, you could check out the Jesus you never knew. You could 'learn something new'.

Are we communicating?

Chapter Five

Discovering A Better Lifestyle

learn the full essence of what it means to be human
learn the full essence of what it means to love and be loved

It appears to me Jesus employed the KISS principle as he taught his students how to be teachers of his relationship lifestyle. "Keep It Short & Simple!" "Keep It Short & Sweet!" And, even the other one, but in a nice way: "Keep It Simple… Stupid!". I'm going to channel the first two in your direction and keep that third one for myself.

In the spirit of keeping it simple I tried to come up with a working class boiled down statement to summarize Jesus' relationship teachings. I wanted it to have a non-religious flavor and be somewhat distinctive. I wanted to cause the listener to 'hear' the message a new and fresh way.

"Try to leave people better off because they met you." That was my best attempt. It is good advice. But still, it sucks when compared to how Jesus summarized his instructions.

He did it much better. He simply said, "treat people the way you want to be treated". Blah Blah Blah. For the people who have Christian church experience we need to get past the Blah Blah Blah. All the extra stuff our church experience taught the 'executive decision maker' to attach to this simple instruction. "First you need to be born again, then you need to be filled with the Spirit, then you need... blah blah blah."

"Treat people the way you want to be treated." This directive will require 'a something extra' for it to work. It appears to be able to stand alone, without needing any help, but that's not true. If it is going to work for you, if you are going to realistically expect the promised intended consequence, then you must 'know' how you want to be treated.

Marvel with me over the genius before us. I have to know how I want to be treated and that will define how I am to treat other people. Genius? Too strong a description... over the top, perhaps? I think I was right on. Have you ever spent time answering that question? Just how do I want to be treated?

My guess is, it would be easier to list the ways I expect to be treated. What if, my version of how I want to be treated, is based on the delusions provided by the Hollywood driven culture? That's a dead end for sure. To be treated like I want almost seems to be just another luxury I know I can't afford. So, I won't even go there. Jesus is telling us we need to go there.

Through the miracle of editing I just saved you about a thousand words of reading. We'll take the shortcut. Let's agree our answer cannot be based on money, or anything else other than, feelings. We can't reciprocate with money. We can with feelings. We need to connect with ourselves and put the feelings we want into words. Visualize. Remember. Capture the good moments.

And, before the shortcut, we recognized giving attention to the Alpha Rules, the internal species directives, helped provide the language, and the imagery, for the way we would like to be treated. We like to be on the receiving end of loving and accepting behaviors; loving and accepting behaviors within the context of satisfying the internal species directives. Once you've nailed the imagery and context down, all that is left would be to make your list and treat other people the same way. Start with your partner and your family. Trust the process. Prove it works. Don't quit. Then expand to your neighbors and friends if they are willing to use the same guidelines. You will create social change within your world. Enjoy!

We're done. You have enough information, should you choose to adopt it, to create great family, enjoy great relationships, regain control of your life, and find peace within yourself. Now for the reality check. Should you start this process remember you are messing with a species survival design feature. Prop 16 stuff. To be successful requires the Adult Rational Mind to re-educate the Executive Decision Maker. This will not be easy like Red Box!

You may find yourself talking to yourself, as if to convince yourself, this fight is worth fighting. That is called 'self talk' and it truly is beneficial. You can make it even better. You and your partner can 'self talk' and 'partner talk'. This helps times ten. The EDM will be aware and it will hear you. Mimic the loving behaviors and it will hear you even better. You can do this.

Application

Agree with your partner to adopt the concept of Lordship to govern your relationship.

Using the Alpha Rules as your guide. Develop a list of loving behaviors that would satisfy these internal drives. Then share your ideas with your partner and rewrite them as necessary. This is a fantastically therapeutic relationship exercise. This may be the first time you ever explored your partners' emotions and feelings. Don't be surprised if you both 'tear up'. Watery eyes speak volumes to a therapist. Don't 'shame up'. Work past that. Take a time out if needed. Just get past it. "Hugs and tears." "Hugs and tears and a relationship for years."

Get to know Jesus. Get to know Jesus with your partner. Discover his phenomenology. Find a modern language red letter version of the Bible. Read the red letters. Those are the words Jesus spoke. Skim and identify. Shim and identify the instructions that speak to relationships and behaviors. Capture the images. Remember Jesus taught in the language and culture of his day. Some examples or applications of a teaching may seem too foreign. In that case focus on the imagery. One of his more effective directives speaks to the issue of 'settling the matter quickly'. The example he provided, for us, may work as a distraction. So, practice focusing on the imagery. Share your interpretation of the imagery with your partner. Load up on options. This is where the communicative magic takes place.

Keep in mind the power of nonverbal communication. Monitor your vocal tones and body expressions. It's better to think you have a long way to go than to think you've arrived.

79

Let tone and body language be your first focus. Smile with your lips, and your eyes, and your voice. "Set the table before you eat. Prepare yourself before you speak." Mentally repeat this admonition before you let words come out of your mouth.

Anticipate the Discovery phenomenon. Until that happens: Practice. Practice. Practice. Work. Work. Work. Hugs and tears. Hugs and tears. Hugs and tears.

Remember to 'unlearn'. Our culture has given us all, 'thinking errors'. You and your partner should commit to observe and examine our culture. "How have these 'waters we swim in' affected us?" I'll give you my short list and you can come up with your own.

I see our television and Hollywood driven culture producing way too many woefully dependent, sex organs with feet, that pursue an unattainable form of happiness, but will settle for escapist behaviors associated with drug use and entertainment frenzy.

You have been affected. Some of that was sure to get on you. And, you are going to have to deal with it.

"Shalom Y'all."

Chapter Six

Surviving the Crisis

is the airplane still flying

There is a philosophy in Crisis Management, which says the very first step is to accurately define the crisis. To that end, it is helpful to ask the question, "Is the airplane still flying?" The pilot understands this is the first question to ask in the event of an inflight emergency. If the plane is still flying, he has time to address the issues related to the cause of the emergency. If it is not flying, then his options are considerably more limited.

The blue collar working class world is in crisis. And, it looks like our 'plane' is in a death spiral. The policies of our government are sucking all the capital out of our monetary system. Borrowed money without the ability to repay is an illusion. To believe anything else is a delusion. When the money is gone it cannot move. When money doesn't move things don't get built. When construction stops we don't work. When we don't work mama is not happy. When mama's not happy nobody is happy.

NO! When money stops moving and there is no work, we starve. Our children will starve. It will be just a matter of time before food stamps become meaningless. Food stamps are a delusion. Food stamps are the corral the cows are put in just before they are slaughtered. Food stamps are not a refuge. Food stamps are a symptom of a greater problem. And, that problem is in front of us now. Our problem… this crisis was created by the people we hired and we trusted. We need to fire them and find a better way.

The blue collar working class relationship world is in crisis. We have been taught to think it normal to exist in a world of broken and dysfunctional relationships. People die alone, and full of anxiety and regrets, never knowing another style of living exists. It shouldn't be that way. You've been affected. I've given you a chance to work the process. Unlearn the bad and relearn the good. Others aren't so fortunate.

The solution to our political and social crisis is overwhelming. It may not be manageable. It may not be survivable. My buddies from work are aware Homeland Security is buying up all the ammunition we need for our guns. The government is doing that for a reason. Nobody needs to tell the blue collar working class to be concerned. We know and we are.

As to the money being skimmed and harvested from us, I don't know where that is going. Maybe somewhere there is a special government compound being built to protect the progressive elite. Maybe they need the ammo to keep us from the food they are stockpiling. I will never know because I don't have a seat at the table. I'm like you, a fetus with no say in the matter.

I hope you heard me just say I do not trust our elected officials and I do not trust the media to provide honest explanations for anything. They can give a thousand people TV face time, each offering a similar explanation, and I will not believe it. I will not accept it. They sold us down the river long ago. They took advantage of our trust and I will not make that mistake again.

I have no confidence in our government or its propaganda machine. Our government, as any government, only can survive through one of two ways. That is, through he confidence of its people or through some form of slavery. I hope I taught you to see this clearly, the psychological warfare being waged on the American people has the intent, and the ability, to enslave us, to harvest us, and make it feel like normal.

I've given you enough information to recognize that. The only 'cultural shift' we need to experience is in the direction of the way it once was; a time when people understood and assumed personal responsibility for their own lives. Not, in the direction the progressives would have it. Sadly, the damage done may be too severe for any legitimate hope for recovery. And, this fact may be their final gambit.

They may hope to scare us into a future we don't want. The consequence of which would make it feel normal to be some kind of farm produce, a thing to be harvested. For the Americans yet to be born, it would be too late. It would almost be impossible for them to recognize how their reality came about, and impossible to comprehend a different life, or create an escape plan to achieve it.

Harvesting Americans requires reality manipulation. We can see their fingerprints all over us. We've adapted to our politicians looking us in the eye and lying to us. We've adapted to accept political spin and political rhetoric as something other than lying. We've adapted to a form of trust that will not question political motive or political wisdom. We've adapted to our national news outlets shaping our understanding of reality by their choices for what kind of information we receive.

We've adapted to the willful deception, which maintains an

artificial gasoline shortage, which inflates the price at the pump and keeps our country underemployed. We will adapt to our health care being treated the same way. We've adapted to the destruction of the American Black Family. We've adapted to the artificially created public perception that allows minority ethic groups to believe the fault lies with the poor and working class white people. We've adapted to the belief the government can provide entitlements that presumes a person born in our country is entitled to the privilege of not taking responsibility for their lives, their choices, and the consequences of their choices.

We've adapted to a form of national censorship we know as political correctness that serves to mold and enslave our thinking. We've adapted to mother's killing their babies as a form of birth control. We've adapted to our politicians working for the special interest groups and we've adapted to the lie that this only occurs with the other political party.

We've adapted to the belief our retirement plans are sound and will be in force when we retire. We've adapted to our government practicing social engineering. We've adapted to the massive amount of debt this social engineering has created without having any real concern for the consequences. We've adapted to paying outrageous taxes to pay for stupid ideas.

We've adapted to our once effective two party system morphing into a one party system. We've adapted to the circus event we know as political campaigns and behave as though we think our voice has a say in the process. We've adapted to believe poor and working class ethic groups are enemies of one another.

We've adapted to believe the status quo will remain forever. Our food source and supply line is a permanent structure and the grocery stores will always be open and the shelves will always be stocked. We've adapted to believe broken relationships and broken families are normal, acceptable, and to be expected. And, worse, we've adapted to believe we are powerless to affect change in our world.

All of our 'adaptations' have contributed to our reality we share. For babies entering the world today, this most certainly will be their 'normal'. If we don't intervene it can only get worse. It may soon come to the place, the poor and working class, are provided sheds to live in and lime green jumpsuits to wear. Our young will adapt to that. Don't allow this to happen.

I would prefer death over willful participation to that end. There are dark clouds on our horizon. Everybody sees it coming. There is a glimmer of hope and that requires the poor and blue collar working class to lock arms and say, "Not On My Watch!" This sliver of hope relies, not so much on us dying, rather in how we vote.

We need to adopt a whole new way of thinking about the voting process.

Are you aware our political leaders tell us what the issues are and then we are told to choose sides? They have proven beyond a reasonable doubt they willfully lie to us and intentionally mislead us. We need to be smarter. We should consider everything they present, every word that leaves their mouth, as deceptive smoke and mirrors. And, we need to tell the new crop of elected officials how to we want our world to work.

We can do our own social engineering. "Just because this is the way it is, doesn't mean it has to be." Remember that. Embrace that. We the people have the power. We just need to adopt a better way to use our power. We cannot afford to continue to give it away blindly. If only for spite we should send them ALL packing. They've done us enough harm.

250 million Americans are in danger. We are horrifically exposed. Should our financial system collapse, we are at risk of starving or worse. Overnight, we become a potential food source. This may not happen, but on the other hand, it might and it could happen in the very near future. One thing for certain, our political leaders and their families are not at risk. I'm not pleased with that. The small percentage of Americans who control most of the wealth are not at risk. I honestly can say, good for them. The species survives. However, I'm not prepared to say, bad for us. We have one last card to play.

If ever we needed one voice, we need it now. If we locked arms, and stayed united, we could influence our destiny, change our fate. We don't have to remain a fetus without a say. Consider this brazen and wild thought. It is so simple. The best things always are.

We could vote ourselves into power. We could control either political party. We don't need a third party. Practically overnight, we could highjack either party and tell whichever one, the way it is to be. We have time, in this election cycle, to elect representatives from our own stockpile of talent. I mean really, how hard can it be? I've had first year apprentices exhibit better sense than Joe Biden and he's been in Washington what, 40 years? Like I said, I would trust 550 working class grandmothers over the gang we have right now. There is no way we could not improve the situation.

We could do this thing. We could send blue collar working class men and women to Washington to speak for us and meet our needs. We could get America working again. We could save America by saving ourselves.

We have simple basic needs. We need to work. We need to NOT watch our children starve and to NOT allow our children to be enslaved. Just about everything else is fluff.

The problem to overcome on the working class side is our lack of ability to communicate with one another. As long as the government does not shut down the internet there will be a way. We have a possible solution and we should use it. I have a social networking website that can be used to get the ball rolling. People a lot smarter than me can do a better job I'm sure. But, on the front-side, if none other is available, mine will work. Alphapeace.com

In my gut, I fear we may be too far gone. We need to prepare for the worse. We need to prepare to survive. If you are hearing me tell you to become a 'prepper' then we are communicating. You need to do everything you can to keep your family from becoming a food source.

And, you need to adopt the Jesus lifestyle, so, in the event you and your family do survive, you will be able to help build the new civilization with the social norms conducive to experiencing the full essence of what it means to be human.

You will be able to pass on to the next generation the skill set that teaches how to do family and make committed long term relationships work. And one more very important thing, the Jesus lifestyle should be the foundation for all the alliances you will need to create during these difficult times. Trust, like food, will be scarce. Plan for it. The Jesus lifestyle will help to make possible the phenomenon of people trusting other people.

We can create a new America and we can create a new future for ourselves. We have a slight, glimmer of a chance. There is reason for hope. We have to wake up, lock arms, and take control... NOW!

You can agree with me or not. No arm twisting. Choose door number one or door number two. Whatever course you choose, this I want you to know, I am not your enemy.

Alphapeace.com A blue collar place to link arms and build healthy relationships.

A Personal Note to Pastors

I want you to consider what I just did for you. I just provided the outreach tool Jesus planned. Your people could benefit. They could learn a better way to do family and a better way to do committed relationships. They could become a more flavorful salt and a more intense light. You could impact your community, in a meaningful way, for Jesus... as he intended. Never, have a people needed the Jesus lifestyle message more than our people, our neighbors, our children, do right now... today.

Your EDM may be telling you to stay the course. Pastors are not immune to Prop 16! I'm asking you to repent, learn something new. Help save people as Jesus would have you to do... save them for today, for this lifetime, as well as for eternity. Help them to become peacemakers within their own lives and within their own family. And, after that, if you still want, you could visit and continue teaching according to your theology and denominational distinctive.

And one more thing, ... I am not your enemy.

Chapter Seven

Key Perspectives and Concepts to Understanding
Your Reality

*your reality is a construction project and you should know
whose been supplying the materials to build it*

For the beginner, our definition for reality usually sounds like, "The way things are". Don't let this definition be enough. I urge you to look into the social microscope. Dig a little deeper. Ask, "How did the way things are, get this way?"

The Blue Collar Manifesto is not an attempt to make you a psychologist. I'm not one. I'm a construction worker with a degree. My counseling degree provides an informed view of counseling theory. The foundation for counseling theory is its understanding of how we learn. And, it follows; some things we 'learn' are neither accurate nor beneficial. Therapists help people recognize this. This cognitive craft helps people to recognize and 'unlearn' the harmful and replace that with the beneficial.

Analogy, comparative word imagery, is often used to explain difficult concepts. I will do that as well because this project is not a dissertation. I'm not shooting for technical accuracy. The language and imagery I use will help you understand how we learn and how our perceptions of reality develop.

89

My first milestone is to convince the poor and blue collar working class men and women, our version of reality is a construction project. We build it. Once we get our head around this, then it will be easier to understand we can demo, or deconstruct, the reality structure we now have and replace it with a better, more successful one.

I'm motivated to do this because the 'science' of building a cultural reality is understood by very powerful and very unfriendly people. They've gotten into your head, and worse. We as individuals, and as a nation, are being currently being harvested. You'll see. Nobody is 'looking out for us'. Once you learn the basics, you can recognize who they are, what they have done, and then you can join me to make them stop.

Prepare yourself to feel betrayed and to be angry. But first, you need to become familiar with some new information. Said another way, I'm going to help you build a new wing onto your existing 'reality interpretation structure'. So, please, just read and absorb. This is your foundation. Build a good one.

Primer

This is the part where I need you to help me help you. Psycho-babble is called that for a reason and it is boring in all its forms. As over-simplified as it is, this chapter will not be an easy read.

I've built in redundancy to help you remember. And, consider this help: Use these three themes for sorting purposes; the adult rational mind, the executive decision maker, and "monkey see monkey do".

The first two are our thinking mechanisms. If I compare them to a computer, the screen would be our adult rational mind or conscious mind and the hard drive would be our executive decision maker or subconscious mind. "Monkey see monkey do" provides the most basic image for how our species learns. This learning feature is more important than you can recognize right now. It has a greater impact than any of us have taken the time to imagine.

Note this: One of the many social skills currently being erased from public memory is the ability to enjoy simple dialogue; the skill set to have meaningful conversation. You will learn faster if you take this opportunity to discuss these precepts with a friend or your relationship partner. This type of conversation I'm advocating has a name. It is called therapeutic dialogue and is a common form of relationship homework.

Here is my suggestion. Read this chapter knowing you may want to come back a few times after you've finished the book. More information will stick than you realize. A second and third read will solidify the information into a working structure.

I'm putting life-changing information in front of you. With this information you will be able to take back control of your life. That said, first you must discover how it is you do not NOW have control. Read on and this will soon become apparent.

The Seven Perspectives:

A perspective is a point of view, a place to stand to see clearer. Just knowing these perspectives exist will help. As you become familiar remember to keep it simple. You are not entering the world of the super complex. Right now, you are just becoming aware.

Species Perspective

You could never hope to acquire an accurate understanding of your reality, or anyone else's for that matter, if you use your own perspective. We are naturally egocentric. We see from the inside out. Our views of the world are filtered by all of our previous conclusions we drew from our life experience.

The most reliable way to know yourself is to know your Species. Humans are the most studied critters on the planet. We have built in design features that govern how we learn. It is our learning mechanism that has enabled us to survive for all these thousands of years.

Our learning mechanism has been identified and turned against us by those skilled in reality manipulation. You need to know what they know because without this information you will most likely adopt and accept the new social structures they have been creating. And, whatever mangled world they present, it will feel like normal to you.

One guiding principle, found within the species perspective is, "if it's good for the species, then it is good for you". And so it follows, "if it's bad for the species, then it is bad for you". This is a small first step. Please tweak your thinking to include this. There exists right now in our culture, publicly accepted social concepts, which have recently been spliced into our sense of normal. They are not good for the individual and they certainly are not good for the species.

Included within a proper species perspective would be the innate survival drives the species provides to its members. Our species has seven basic survival functions. They've worked well for over forty thousand years. These internal species directives are your best source, for the information you need, to build a life worth living. Later, an entire section will be given to these survival rules.

Historical Perspective

This perspective helps you recognize 'things were not always this way'. Our social environment continues to evolve. Let's look at the pre-modern era. This period spans from before the ancient world until roughly the end of the dark ages, around 1400 A.D. During these times societies were 'closed', meaning there was not much outside influence. The clan culture or the village culture was set and social change might not occur for hundreds of years.

The modern era ranges from the end of the dark ages until around the end of World War 2. The Renaissance, a French word meaning new birth, marks the beginning. This era brought with it a move to larger cities, the elevated status of higher learning, as well as a sense that science and commerce will solve all of man's problems. New worlds were being discovered and new ways of thinking were invading every community. The village culture was overtaken by this new world order.

In the 1960's, the term post-modern started to work its way through society. It is believed the threat of nuclear annihilation caused the public to question whether science really can solve all of mankind's problems. "What good is it if science finds a cure for every disease if only later to kill us all with the weapons of mass destruction it created?" Post-modern thought gives each of us permission to question everything. My advice to you is to do just that. "Just because this is the way it is NOW doesn't mean it has ALWAYS been this way."

Systems Perspective

Systems theory makes the complex easier to understand.

Physicians use it to diagnose. Electricians use it to troubleshoot. Sociologists use it to understand how a society developed. Marriage and Family therapists use it when applying their craft to help folks like us. You use it to figure out why your lawn mower won't start or your favorite recipe didn't turn out. The inverse is also true. When you follow the recipe correctly, you can trust the outcome to be as planned.

Systems theory operates off of one core premise. "Whatever is happening in the system right now, the system is perfectly designed to produce that result." Systems theory is the study of influence and consequences. It begins by asking the question, "If what I'm experiencing now is a consequence, then what are the 'influence factors,' which caused this to be."

Once you've established the 'why and how' a system is behaving as it is, then should you choose, you can change the outcome by introducing new 'influence factors' into the system. The outcome cannot remain the same as before. New influence factors guarantees new consequences.

In social systems, every person acts and operates as an 'influence factor'. When the reality manipulators game the learning mechanism of Americans on a national scale, they don't expect immediate success with all of us. They don't need too. If their top down message remains consistent, you and I will soon play a role.

We will influence each other. The simple fact any new message has been adopted by other members of our social circle will cause us to consider its validity. And, as you will soon discover, we can adopt a belief without truly analyzing it for beneficial consequences. Once a thing gives the appearance of normal the deal is practically done.

Structure Perspective

Think of this as applied systems theory. There is a whole wing of counseling theory dedicated to structural influence. "Structure affects behavior." "Change the structure, change the behavior".

Structure can be cognitive. This would be the sub-conscious mental rules and tools you acquired and trust to get through life successfully. Structure can be social as seen in our customs and cultural and behavioral norms. It can be legal. Perhaps the most effective way to quickly alter social structure is to pass a law outlining a new way for society to think and behave.

Some forms of structure will lend credibility to the message. Progressive democrats like Harry Reid are given TV face time to tell Americans how to think. When he says the Tea Party views are extreme and way outside of mainstream America, he is not just your average Joe running his mouth at work. He is talking on television.

The social structure of Television is that it has been the chief public information injection system since its inception. Television has been in our homes before most of us were born. We've learned from it all of our lives. The trust factor is very high.

A strange thing exists about our relationship with television. Our roles have been defined. Television speaks and we listen without being allowed to talk back and ask questions. We have been conditioned to hear whatever message comes to us through that electronic box. Most of the messages arrive in the form of entertainment. Many of today's program story lines depict real life situations. The writers invent the personalities of the characters.

If we are watching a drama type program, it will be written in real world life like situations. We are affected by the invented forms of 'normal' we witness. Unfortunately, the writers like to push the envelope and spice up the drama. Not just one show. Every show. There is an extremely unhealthy amount of violence and infidelity and sexual expression on television; as well as, just about all other forms of entertainment. Can you see how vulnerable that makes us? Television, as well as movies, not only borrows from our culture, **it reshapes** our culture. And, the people living in the culture will adapt, ever so quietly, to the images it presents.

Television should be called the Bias Transfer Delivery System. Historically, television news, commentary, and program content has had a distinct liberal/progressive bias. Television became their 'go to' tool to cause us to adopt their views. Harry Reid is just another voice, in a long line of voices and images, which have said things to affect how you think and to bring you around to their way of thinking.

There are times when the political actors given television face time, defy logic. Nancy Pelosi told the American people "we have to pass the bill in order to know what's in it". This is what I heard her say, "I'm the dumbest woman on the face of the planet but that doesn't matter. I have the power of the press and control of television news and commentary. And, there isn't anything you can do about it".

Sometimes, the content of a TV show is politically biased. This will be perceived, at best, as an option for 'normal' thinking. Everyone watching will be affected. Everyone watching will have their sense of reality manipulated.

Other social structures have a great deal of influence. Labor unions and the like are a type of social structure. The progressive democrats have a history of enjoying organized labor as an 'in their pocket' demographic. They should thank us better. Some members of organized labor work very hard for them. They are very vocal about their political views. And, by their behaviors, within this social structure, they create a great deal of influence and power.

Physical structures are built to last. So are the social and legal ones. Try to recognize the message within the influence and the structure that propels it. The next time you and your partner watch a TV show, try to identify the message and influence the structure of television brings into your world. You will never run out of conversation topics once you start to recognize the nature of the content being leveled at you. You won't want the 'normal' as presented through television.

Message Perspective

This is applied structural perspective. You and I were born into a world unlike any other time in human history. Never before has communication been so instantaneous. The communication industry, the providers of television, internet, cell phone, and the like, play a major role in affecting thinking and behavioral norms. The influence is in the message.

Progressive democrats like Harry Reid are given TV face time to tell Americans how to think. When he says the Tea Party views are extreme and way outside of mainstream America, what message did you hear? I bet you didn't hear a list of Tea Party views or reasons why they should be considered extreme or outside mainstream America. The message was, "Pay them no mind, they're dumb and we don't need what they are selling".

The nonverbal facial expression serves to underscore and reinforce the verbal message. His every reason for being in front of the camera, at this time, on national television, is to instill a bias against the Tea Party view. He can do this without us knowing anything about their political beliefs. His message is designed to make you prejudice. We don't need to be taught how to be prejudice. We need to know our elected officials are making wise decisions for us.

An awful thing happens when Americans adapt to dumbed down messages. We get politicians not quite smart enough to understand the message they are presenting. When Obama tells a group of Hispanics to "remember who your friends are", what is the message they heard? It wasn't "love thy neighbor" I promise you! It was, "you can't trust the white people". "The rich white Republicans who do not like Hispanics." It doesn't matter if that is true or not. The intended consequence is to get the Hispanic vote.

The unintended consequence is to stimulate aggressive behavior toward unsuspecting, and just as confused, white poor and working class. They are like every other 'ethic' in this regard. White working class have the same goals. We are just doing our best to keep a roof over our head and food on the table. 99.99 % of poor and working class white people are not the enemy of anybody. We don't have the time nor the energy for bigotry. The 1950's are over. We get it. We're like most everybody else… a mixture of rude and friendly.

You may have heard political pundits give commentary. Oftentimes you will hear the observation, "he needs to stay on message". A political message is a carefully contrived verbal illusion attempting to cause you to focus an a single political issue. These usually follow a familiar and predictable script.

The message will tell you what the problem is, [which may not even be the most pressing problem the nation is facing] then they will scare you away from the opponents proposed solution. Usually their version of the opponents proposed solution doesn't resemble anything the opponent would recognize. Then, they will cement the connection between you and them. We are a team. We're in this together.

I know this in our normal. I get it. That is my point. We should not allow it.

The Illusion Perspective

Magicians prove people can be tricked. No one is exempt. Everybody can be fooled. Professional perception manipulators know how to trick the way you perceive your reality. They can sell you 'sizzle' when you wanted to buy 'steak'. And, worse, they can take your money and convince you the aroma you smell is what you were really looking for. Think not? Do an inventory on why you believe what you do and why you trust those you do. You might find your reasons to be, illusive.

Everything, everything, everything is an illusion. All of your life experience takes place within a small region inside your brain. People go to college to learn how this works. You could earn a PhD in this field. Like magicians, they can trick you. They know how to keep 'the elephant in the room' invisible.

This perspective provides a sense of balance. It gives us a platform to work off of. We all like to try to figure out how the magician tricked us. What you should do is transfer this curiosity over to your working belief system. Once you learn the following terms and concepts, ask the same question, "How did they trick me?"

The My Worth Perspective

Your worth to the species is equal to everyone else. There is no one born better than you. Social convention tries to convince us there are some among us who are our 'betters'. That belief only works if you allow it.

When it comes to the 'haves' and the 'have not's the poor and working class are clearly in with the 'have not's. Get your head around this. There is a distinction between having less and being less. Our Species has a wicked sense of humor in this regard. Most of the things the 'haves' possess do not contribute to the overall quality of living as the species defines, quality of life. The upside is, once you recognize what is important to the species, in order to have a full and contented life, your transition will be much much easier!

And, do not allow yourself to cower in the presence of powerful people. Powerful people behave like large burly bullies. I've never witnessed, or even heard of large burly bullies withstand the wrath of a mob of angry little guys. There are more of us than them. Remember, just because you have less does not mean you are less. And, remember this too, there are way more of us than them. Once we know the rules, and once we lock arms, we can create a reality that works much better for us. We can push the reset button. We can reshape things.

Terms and Concepts

Every job you've ever had came with a specialized 'language'. You needed to learn the terms and concepts associated with your job. Otherwise, you could not communicate efficiently with your boss or your co-workers. We're doing the same thing here. The first term to learn will be the only big word I use. Understanding the concept is more important than knowing how to pronounce it!

Phenomenological

This term combines two familiar words: phenomenon and logic. The intent is to describe human reality. A person's logic is a phenomenon based on their interpretation, the meaning and value they applied, to all of their life experiences. This is what you need to know. Human babies are not born with instincts to tell us the best and proper way to do this thing we call, life. Your personal 'rules and tools', your personal logic, was constructed all by yourself. No doubt you had outside influence, both friendly and otherwise.

The important thing to take from this is that you are a phenomenon. In the big picture of human existence you are a living experiment. "What would happen if I put this baby, in this family, in this socio-economic environment, with this particular array of personal, cultural, and legal influence?" You can track your life this way. You can see how outside influence has affected the adult you became.

The First Birth

Around the beginning of the seventh month, while you developed within the womb, an amazing human design feature came upon you. As if a light switch was flipped, a supremely special event occurred. You became aware. Sensory perception began to inform the brain; first with hearing and touch, and later after leaving the womb, taste and smell and then sight.

There was a time when the beginning of the third trimester was the boundary line for the abortion timetable. After that the baby has conscious awareness. It is beneficial to see the onset of consciousness as your first birth. Your phenomenology begins at this moment. Your mother most likely has a different opinion! That said, when compared to all that is associated with you becoming aware, leaving the womb is just a formality. You could not experience anything, any aspect of life without it. Being aware means you know you exist, you can experience life, you think therefore you are.

The Executive Decision Maker

Psychologists have long understood your adult rational mind is not your executive decision maker. Shocking as it may sound, this is great news. You have within you two thinking mechanisms; one of which we are familiar and one that requires an introduction. Fair enough?

In the womb, at your first birth, when the senses began to collect and report data to the brain, the early framework for your executive decision maker was already up and running. This is a fantastic species survival tool. Without it learning of any kind could not take place. Without it we simply could not survive. "The EDM" or executive decision maker quietly helps you adapt to your world. Other names you may have heard might be the Mind, the Self, the Sub-conscious, the Consciousness, or the Inner Child.

This aspect of you, once online, is working 24/7 everyday of your life. I'll provide one very common example. Most of have experienced this or something similar. Remember when a friend was horsing around and threw an object toward your head. Let's say it was a chalkboard eraser. OK, for the rest of the world, let's say it was a whiteboard eraser. Either way, this thing was rocketing toward the side of your head. In an instant, without thinking, or so we have been led to believe, by some form of reflex action, you were able to evade or knock it out of the way.

Actually, the EDM came to the rescue. The senses reported enough information to register imminent danger. An escape plan was developed and initiated. Everything we needed was accomplished without informing the rational mind until after the fact. The child's rational mind created its own version. "Only by MY super hero like reflex was I able to foil this evil plot!" Not so.

The EDM has features similar to computer programming. However, the difference lies in that it writes the program, and uploads the content, on the fly. When you joked about being a 'work in progress' you were speaking the truth. Here's the basics. The senses report everything they are designed to recognize. This information is immediately defined, sorted, and stored in such a way that it can be later grouped with things it sees as similar or recalled in the form of a memory or added to later to expand its meaning.

If we saw this process as a flow chart, the first stop for the sensory information would be the 'definition station'. The sensory input has to be interpreted. It has to be given a meaning. And, since we did not arrive with a pre-set glossary to help us with the definitions, we have to come up with our own. And, we do. That is an amazing human design feature, is it not? You might want to sit back and chew on this awhile. Think of the last baby you saw staring at her hand. Was she watching her fingers move? A lot of construction work was going on!

The Adult Rational Mind

This thinking mechanism takes the information provided by the EDM and makes conscious decisions within the context of real time, in the moment, events. Said another way, the adult rational mind helps us to react to whatever issue or situation that is in front of us. However, the adult rational mind is much more than an extension of the executive decision maker. The adult rational mind has another amazing design feature.

All of us make mistakes. All of us have witnesses who can testify to this fact. Our EDM did not get it right every time. Some of its definitions and 'rules and tool's for doing life have shown themselves to be flawed. This results in bad information, known as thinking errors, which begins the process for, unintended, or even bad consequences. Once the adult rational mind recognizes the problem, it has the means to reeducate the EDM. This is great news!

Thinking Errors

Without a doubt, the root cause for practically every issue presented to a Counselor or Therapist would fall under the heading, Thinking Error. The EDM does not get it right every time. However, it will show itself to be exceedingly stubborn to admit it is wrong. Remember the EDM operates like a computer program. It measures reality within the context of the existing program. The one it wrote!! It trusts all its observations, definitions, and conclusions to be true, accurate, and trustworthy. It does not like to be questioned nor seen to be wrong.

Go figure. Most of the elements of your relationship rules and tools were adopted before you were six years old. This is where the 'inner child' language came from. So don't be surprised, in this social climate, almost everyone has relationship, as well as other 'how to do life', thinking errors.

The EDM uses a special tool to deflect and camouflage its responsibility when suspected to be wrong. We know it as 'shame'. Like a skunk it will spray the Adult Rational Mind as if to say, "back off!" A light dose we feel as embarrassment. A heavy dose sets off the fight or flight mechanism. A sustained dose suggests serious problems.

**Therapists have noticed it not unusual for a client to "shame up" as they explore their rules and tools for doing life. Try to not allow this to stop your search. Recognize and embrace it if it does. It means you are on the right track.

Proposition 16

This relates to thinking errors and EDM stubbornness. Carl Rogers was voted by his peers to be the second most influential psychologist of the 20th Century. He developed 19 propositions about the Self. Consider number 16: "Any experience which is inconsistent with the organization of the structure of the self may be perceived as a threat, and the more of these perceptions there are, the more rigidly the self structure is organized to maintain itself." I know I'm right, and I'm not so sure about you right now, so back off!

The 'organization of the structure' are the rules and tools the EDM developed to match what is perceived to be the thinking and behaving requirements within its living environment. These are survival rules and tools. To challenge them will be perceived as a threat and it will respond proportionately to the level of perceived threat.

The classic commercial showing two men arguing over the greatest attribute of their favorite beer, pokes fun at this design feature. "Tastes great!" "Less filling!" Whenever people argue you can trust Prop 16 is involved.

** Let's analyze the beer argument. It began as a simple difference of opinion. However, it was in the way they presented their opinion that 'called in the Marines'. It was the hostile gesturing, along with the elevated and threatening vocal tones, which communicated a 'real and present danger'. The tastes great-less filling argument quickly took a back seat. As it has been observed, "the evil which slumbers within us has been awakened". One more big mess for the Adult

105

Rational Mind to deal with!!

Discovery

This is great news. The primary objective of the EDM is to help you acclimate to the living environment so you can survive. The EDM is stubborn but it is not stupid. If it recognizes a more successful way to think or behave it has the ability to rewrite the code and change our rules and tools survival kit.

The term for this is, Discovery. Sometimes, when the code is rewritten, it is believed we may actually feel the event. I suppose you've had an "ah ha" moment. Or, in the midst of turmoil, you had a 'moment of clarity'. What you felt was your rules and tools survival kit being revamped.

Then again, sometimes the EDM will appear both stubborn and stupid. It will not recognize that which is painfully obvious to everyone else. Sometimes, it will take enduring disastrous consequences just to get its attention. Still, disaster is no guarantee for change to follow. The developed rules and tools are a powerful survival mechanism. When the EDM came online it anticipated getting it right the first time. In our present day culture, to do that, to get it right the first time, is next to impossible.

The Mimic Witness

Long before the baby can talk, the EDM is hard at work monitoring everything. It came with a 'to do' list. We all have 'internal species directives' which assist in giving value, a hierarchy of importance, to the massive amounts of sensory input. In short, the EDM is always in a search mode to find out just what is the proper and the best way to live here.

Have you ever seen a baby mimic adult behavior? That image says it all. The baby is telling us what it is learning. Teenagers and adults do the exact same thing. If you want to know what it is you have learned, your rules and tools, then track what it is you are actually doing as opposed to what it is you say or think you are doing.

Social Proofing

The EDM came online preprogramed to survive, to seek a positive connection with other people, to reproduce, and to assist the young to acclimate into this new environment. It will always blend these internal directives with the rules and tools it has adopted. You and I carry another design feature we cannot escape. It a sense it is a paradox. We seek a thing that does not exist. We are looking for, 'Normal'. Beginning as a baby, and even as an adult, we measure the accuracy of our interpretations of normal by how that mimicked behavior is accepted within our social circle.

The EDM will adjust our behavior to match that which it perceives to be normal within the current social environment. But, understand this. The EDM makes no distinction between fact or fiction, fantasy or concrete, television or real world. It will be influenced by every bit of stimuli and groupings of stimuli regardless of the originators intention. It seeks to hear the 'message'. It assumes it to be accurate. Oh yeah, another thing. When the EDM receives a message that it has already installed within its rules and tools, the repeated interpretation will act as a validation of accuracy for the previous interpretation. Apply these facts to the amount of television you've watched over your lifetime! Scary.

Modeling

Applied social proofing: a technique to intentionally expose the EDM to another way to think or behave. It is effective in all age groups. The premise is simple. Make the EDM aware of a prescribed way to think and repeat this message often, more often, and still more often. Politicians like to hammer home talking points, full of imagery praising themselves, while diminishing their opponent. The reason for the constant barrage of high image advertising during a campaign is simple. It works.

Progressive democrats like Harry Reid are given TV face time to tell Americans how to think. When he says the Tea Party views are extreme and way outside of mainstream America, who was he's talking too? The Adult Rational Mind or the EDM? The Executive Decision Maker of course. He is employing modeling behaviors anticipating the introjection phenomenon to kick in.

Once enough people buy into a message, it will appear to those sitting on the fence, as though the message is now the new normal. The Adult Rational Mind would not think like this, but the EDM would. It was designed to think this way.

We always hear the message. Even if our adult rational mind does not agree with it, we cannot escape being affected. We may not always be convinced. However, we will always be affected.

Culture

The more accurate understanding of culture is, 'the common behaviors and thinking patterns which express the sense of community normal'. If we were fish, culture would be the water we swim in. This sense of normal is transmitted or passed down from one generation to the next. Culture, said another way, is public memory. A culture, or community normal, is absorbed by our youth as they are influenced by the rules and tools modeled within the community.

Culture provides to the EDM the template to adopt and mimic. Freud used a term, introjection, to describe a learning mechanism, which allows us to introject, or adopt without critical analysis, whole segments of observed behavior and incorporate it into our rules and tools for living. This learning mechanism was very useful for most of our species existence. In our current social environment this design feature can and does cause problems. If anyone is interested in finding the source for their thinking errors, the message of our culture is the best place to begin. Examine the water we swim in.

Values

Values are a subset of culture. Where other areas may be deemed optional or less important, values are visibly held to an almost sacred level within the community. When we hear the expression, Family Values, we are hearing about a subset of culture, which has identified the best 'normal' way to do family. This group of thinking and behaving norms has proven themselves to produce the most successful whole life experience. When we hear about 'an attack' on Family Values we are being informed there is an attempt to reduce the cultural importance associated with these special 'how to do family' rules and tools.

This will be repeated. These special rules and tools for enjoying a successful, long term, committed relationship are being erased from public memory. It will take only one generation, failing to pass on to the next, this special grouping of behaviors, thoughts, and feelings, for it to be lost forever.

If you were raised in a broken home, then you most likely do not know the rules or have the tools. You, no doubt, have a sense of normal about the way you do family. But, what you have cannot produce the results we all most want to achieve, a successful whole life experience.

You have values today. The question becomes, "what are they?" Another important question is, "how did you acquire them?" In the context of perception manipulation you really do want to find out. You may, and most likely do, now hold values that do nothing to satisfy the internal species directives. In this case, you will have adopted or adapted to a form of social poison. You would do well to get them out of your system.

This also relates to marriage. I believe people fall 'out of love' and give up on a survivable relationship when their 'how to do relationship' rules and tools are laced with relationship breaking behaviors. This should give everyone pause.

Relationship breaking behaviors will feel normal and will produce results that will also feel normal. This is a sucky situation because the relationship partners are clueless; they cannot see their reality clearly. They cannot recognize how they each contribute to their own problems. Their EDM will define the problem, and offer solutions, using the same structure that helped create it. It is a sucky situation for everyone involved.

Scripts and Response Patterns

These types of cognitive structures speak to basically the same thing. The EDM likes to take shortcuts to help it get through the day without having to keep reinventing the wheel. Once we prove an interaction to be successful then we create a template to use in a future and similar circumstance. The template becomes a script just as if you were a Hollywood actor. When we run into a friend we have a script, already in the cue, to greet our friend. "Hello", "Hey", "Howdy",

"WatzzzzUp". We have scripts for most of our verbal and nonverbal behaviors.

Response patterns are scripted also, just longer. Should the EDM perceive it to be in a hostile environment, it will pull out the set of scripted behaviors it believes necessary. How about a loving environment? Same. It will match the environment with its version of a positive response pattern that it believes has historically produced a successful outcome. Doesn't mean it guarantees a successful outcome, it just believes it will.

Our 'go to' scripts and response patterns often 'just appear' in our behavior and the adult rational mind is left to 'manage' the bad situations these perception shortcuts will sometimes create. Soon, you will have the knowledge to intervene and help re-educate your EDM. The key will be found in the 'consequence'. If the consequence is as successful as you like, then don't change it. If it isn't, then you will have new intervention tools to create a better one.

Reality Manipulation

Reality manipulation is a willful attempt to alter the way another person perceives and operates within their world. We live in an era, and country, which has the knowledge and message injection system (television, radio, texting, etc.) to do this. All that is required is a clear and compelling message, the injection system, and time for the process to work.

This happens everyday. We watch a news report one night and hear the message. We go to work the next day and mimic or repeat the message to our coworkers. They heard the same thing so we 'prove' to each other the legitimacy of the message. Then, at home we watch the same news story repeated. Now, this time, our interpretation of the original message is validated. So it happens, our view of reality was

111

changed. And we didn't even blink.

As a people, we've accepted television, its content and advertising, as a norm. Most Americans do not think this medium to be a threat. The fact is, television is the most influential social change agent since man first walked upright. And, it has been used against us, we all have been harmed, yet because it feels normal, we will not give it a second thought. We are designed this way.

All of the associated television content we allow into our living room has shaped our views of 'normal'. Overall, from a species perspective, this current batch of content is not healthy for the individual or the species. Political activists with the progressive agenda have done us the most harm.

For now, remember this information is your foundation for taking control of your life. You now have the tools to identify the reasons you believe and feel and act like you do. The question becomes whether or not any of your beliefs contribute to the life problems you are experiencing. With a little practice you can learn that for yourself.

One more thought, the foundation you now have should be helpful to recognize the value of a relationship therapist. If you and your partner have fully processed this information, and take that knowledge with you into a counseling session, the work of the therapist will make more sense to you and be more effective.

www.ingramcontent.com/pod-product-compliance
Lightning Source LLC
Chambersburg PA
CBHW060416290526
45791CB00002B/769